SLAVOJ ŽIŽEK/F. W. J. VON SCHELLING

THE ABYSS
OF FREEDOM/
AGES OF
THE WORLD

An essay by Slavoj Žižek
with the text of
Schelling's *Die Weltalter* (second draft, 1813)
in English translation by Judith Norman

Ann Arbor
The University
of Michigan
Press

Copyright © by the University of Michigan 1997
All rights reserved
Published in the United States of America by
The University of Michigan Press
Manufactured in the United States of America
∞ Printed on acid-free paper
2000   1999   1998   1997   4   3   2   1

*A CIP catalog record for this book is available
from the British Library*

Library of Congress Cataloging-in-Publication Data

Žižek, Slavoj.
    The abyss of freedom / Slavoj Žižek. Ages of the world / F.W.J.
von Schelling.
        p.   cm. – (The body, in theory)
    "An essay by Slavoj Žižek with the text of Schelling's Die
Weltalter (second draft, 1813) in English translation by Judith
Norman."
    Includes bibliographical references.
    ISBN 0-472-09652-4 (cloth : alk. paper). – ISBN 0-472-06652-8
(pbk. : alk. paper)
    1. Schelling, Friedrich Wilhelm Joseph von, 1775–1854. Weltalter.
2. Ontology.   3. Absolute, The.   4. Free will and determinism.
5. History – Philosophy.   6. Idealism, German.   7. Psychoanalysis.
8. Lacan, Jacques, 1901–   I. Schelling, Friedrich Wilhelm
Joseph von, 1775–1854.   Weltalter.   English.   II. Title.
III. Title: Ages of the world.   IV. Series.
B2894.W42E5   1997
111—DC21   96-51746
                                                                 CIP

THE ABYSS OF FREEDOM
Slavoj Žižek

I

Perhaps the best-known single line from film noir is the final remark of the doomed hero in Edgar G. Ulmer's *Detour:* "Fate or some mysterious force can put the finger on you or me for no good reason at all." This parlance provides a concise expression of the central enigma Friedrich Wilhelm Joseph von Schelling (1775–1854) struggled to resolve throughout his long philosophical career – the enigma of freedom, of the sudden suspension of the "principle of sufficient reason," discernible from God's radically contingent act of creation up to the "irrational" insistence of a stubborn child on a seemingly trifling point, on which, however, he is ready to stake everything. Schelling's solution involves an unheard-of reversal of the very terms of this enigma: what if the thing to be explained is not freedom but the emergence of the chains of reason, of the causal network – or, to quote Schelling himself: "The whole world is thoroughly caught in reason, but the question is: how did it get caught in the network of reason in the first place?"[1]

Nowhere is the endeavor to comprehend this enigma more strenuous than in the three drafts of *Die Weltalter* ("Ages of the World") from 1811 to 1815. For many years, the third draft, from 1815, was the only one known to exist; it was published in volume 8 of Schelling's *Works* edited by his son, Karl, immediately after the philosopher's death.[2] The two previous drafts were discovered at the end of World War II in the debris of the Munich University library, destroyed by the Allied bombings; they were published in 1946.[3] The three drafts remain fragments: all of them contain only book I of the planned trilogy of "Past," "Present," and "Future." They are interrupted at the crucial point of giving an account of the differentiation between Past and Present, of the emergence of the Word from the self-enclosed rotary motion of drives. However, in their very failure, they are arguably the acme of German Idealism and, simultaneously, a breakthrough into an unknown domain whose contours became discernible only in the aftermath of German Idealism. This breakthrough is most tangible in the second draft, and for this reason it was chosen for translation in the present volume. The work bears witness to such an effort of thought that it is almost painful to read.

A SYSTEM OF FREEDOM

The philosophical system Schelling was working on from about 1807, after abandoning his earlier project of the so-called philosophy of identity, provides an exemplary case of the *noncontemporaneity of a thought to its time,* that is, of the paradoxical temporality in which staying behind coincides with being ahead. In its time, the predominant perception of this system was of a hopelessly outdated regression to premodern theosophy. It is now clear that the entire post-Hegelian constellation – from Marxism to the existentialist notion of finitude and temporality as the ultimate horizon of being, from deconstructionist "decentering" of the self-presence of *logos* to New Age obscurantism – has its roots in Schelling's late philosophy.

Schelling's late philosophy should by no means be reduced to a mere "intermediate" phenomenon, announcing the contours of future thought in the inadequate language of the past. It rather functions as a kind of vanishing mediator, designating a unique constellation in which, for a brief moment after the disintegration of Absolute Idealism, something became visible that, once so-called post-Hegelian thought settled itself, and found shape in the guise of Schopenhauer, Marx, and Nietzsche, was again lost from sight. Schelling alone persisted in the "impossible" position of the post-Idealist crack that was quickly filled by the post-Hegelian "reversals" of Idealism. Schelling's first name for this crack is the gap that forever separates Existence from its Ground, that is, the rational, articulated universe of the divine Word (*logos*) from that which in God himself is not God, from the contraction of the impenetrable Real that provides the support for the expansion of the divine Word.

Against all false appearances and even occasional misformulations by Schelling himself, this gap that separates Existence from its Ground has nothing whatsoever to do with the premodern duality of "cosmic principles" (Light and Darkness, Masculine and Feminine, etc.). There is an eternal temptation to supplement the standard idealist edifice with such a duality of principles; insofar as Plato was the first idealist, no wonder that one of the obsessions of the New Age approach is to unearth – beneath Plato's public teaching at our disposal in his written dialogues – his true, esoteric doctrine. This "secret teaching" offers an exemplary case of the *theoretical* obscene Other that accompanies, as a shadowy double, the One of pure theory. On a closer look, the positive *content* of this secret teaching reveals itself to be pop-wisdom commonplaces à la Joseph Campbell sold in thousands at airport bookstores, New Age platitudes about the duality of cosmic principles: the One, the positive principle of Light, must be accompanied by primordial Otherness, the mysterious dark principle of feminine matter . . . Therein resides the basic paradox: the secret we are supposed to discern through the arduous work of textual archaeology is none other than the most notorious New Age pop wisdom – a nice example of the Lacanian topology in which the innermost kernel coincides with the radical externality. Here is simply another chapter in the eternal fight waged by obscurantist Illumination against Enlightenment: insofar as Plato was the first great Enlightener, the obsession with Plato's secret teaching bears witness to an effort to prove that Plato himself was an obscurantist preaching a special initiatic doctrine.[4]

In spite of its theosophical flavor, Schelling's difference between Existence and its Ground radically undermines every dualism of cosmological "principles." The central tenet of Schelling's "Philosophical Investigations into the Essence of Human Freedom," which immediately precedes *Weltalter* and announces its problematic,[5] is that if one is to account for the possibility of Evil, one has to presuppose a split of the Absolute itself into God insofar as he fully exists and the obscure, impenetrable Ground of his Existence. With characteristic speculative audacity, Schelling locates the split that opens up the possibility of Evil in God himself. This distinction between God's Existence and its Ground, between the Absolute insofar as it fully exists, insofar as it is posited as such, illuminated by the Light of Reason, and the

Absolute qua obscure longing (*Sehnsucht*) that strives for something outside itself without a clear notion of what it strives for, means that God is not fully "himself" – that there is something in God that isn't God. In "Philosophical Investigations," this relationship between the obscure Will of the Ground and the illuminated, effectively existing Will is not yet thought through, so that Schelling's position is here, strictly speaking, contradictory. That is to say, his answer to the question "What does the obscure Will aspire to?" is: it strives after illumination, it yearns for the Word to be pronounced. If, however, the obscure Will of the Ground itself aspires to *logos,* in what precise sense is it then *opposed* to it? *Weltalter* resolves this contradiction by qualifying the first Will as the divine *Selbstheit,* "being-itself," as the contractive force that actively opposes the Light of Reason and thereby serves as the necessary ground of the latter's expansion.

However, already in "Philosophical Investigations" Schelling's position is more subtle than may appear: this obscure-impenetrable side of God, the Ground of his Existence, is *not* to be conceived as a positive Base, the true foundation of Being, with Reason as its parasitic accident: the Ground is in itself ontologically hindered, hampered, its status is in a radical sense *preontological* – it only "is" *sous rature,* in the mode of its own withdrawal. The only true Substance is God in his actual Existence, and *Grund* is ultimately a name for God's self-deferral, for that elusive X which lacks any proper ontological consistency, yet on account of which God is never fully himself, cannot ever attain full self-identity. God needs this foreign body in his heart since without this minimum of contractive force, he wouldn't be "himself" – what, paradoxically, forever prevents God from attaining full self-identity is the very impenetrable kernel of his *Selbstheit.* This tension in the midst of the Absolute itself is, therefore, far more enigmatic than it may appear, since it is thoroughly incompatible with the oppositions that define the space of traditional ontology: the opposition between Ground and Existence does not overlap with the opposition between mere possibility and actuality (if this were the case, Ground couldn't corrode from within the self-identity of actual Existence); it is not simply a new name for the duality of the Real and the Ideal in Schelling's early philosophy, that is, for the symmetrical polarity of two ontological principles (the Ground is "less" than Existence, it lacks full ontological consistency); it definitely doesn't imply that Ground is in any way the "true substance" or "foundation" of Reason. The enigma resides in the fact that Ground is ontologically nonaccomplished, "less" than Existence, but it is precisely as such that it corrodes from within the consistency of the ontological edifice of Existence. In other words, Schelling first opposes Existence (the fully actual God) and the mere Ground of Existence (the blind striving that lacks actuality) as the Perfect and the Imperfect, and then goes on to treat the two as complementary and to conceive true completeness as the unity of the two, as if the Perfect itself needs the Imperfect in order to assert itself. *This is why there is Evil in the world: on account of the perverse need of the Perfect for the Imperfect,* as if the intersection of the Perfect and the Imperfect is more perfect than the Perfect itself.

This paradoxical need of the Perfect for the Imperfect is another name for the Hegelian project of conceiving the Absolute "not only as Substance, but also as Subject." That is to say, what one should always bear in mind is that, in the opposition between (imperfect) Ground and (perfect) Existence, *Subject is on the side of Ground qua imperfect: subject* designates the "imperfection" of Substance, the inherent gap, self-deferral, distance-from-itself, which forever prevents Substance from fully realizing itself, from becoming "fully itself." The fact that there is something in God that is not God means that Substance implies Subject as its constitutive openness, gap. This also throws new light on the ontological status of sexual difference: Schelling explicitly sexualizes the relationship between Existence and its Ground, conceiving Ground as the impenetrable "feminine" foundation of the male Word. As such, Ground must remain in the background, silent: the moment Ground usurps the leading role, it changes from a beneficient protective power to a horrible fury bent on destroying every determinate Existence. It is easy to recognize here the standard patriarchal fear of the destructive force of fully asserted femininity. There is, however, another, perhaps unexpected conclusion to be drawn from this: is this radical negativity bent on destroying every determinate Existence not the very kernel of subjectivity? Does this not mean that *subjectivity is, in its most basic dimension, in an unheard-of way, "feminine"?* Insofar as "subject" is the Ground that asserts itself "as such," in the very medium of Existence, against every determinate form of actual existence, subject is a potentiality, never fully actualized, and the feminine Ground asserted against the "masculine" existence-logos.

This basic insight of Schelling whereby, prior to its assertion as the medium of rational Word, the subject is the pure "night of the Self," the "infinite lack of being," the violent gesture of contraction that negates every being outside itself, also forms the core of Hegel's notion of madness: when Hegel determines madness as withdrawal from the actual world, the closing of the soul into itself, its "contraction," the cutting-off of its links with external reality, he all too quickly conceives this withdrawal as a "regression" to the level of the "animal soul" still embedded in its natural environs and determined by the rhythm of nature (night and day, etc.). Does this withdrawal, on the contrary, not designate the severing of the links with the *Umwelt*, the end of the subject's immersion in its immediate natural surroundings, and is it as such not the founding gesture of "humanization?" Was this withdrawal into self not accomplished by Descartes in his universal doubt and reduction to cogito, which, as Derrida pointed out in his "Cogito and the History of Madness,"[6] also involves a passage through the moment of radical madness? Are we thus not back at the well-known passage from *Jenaer Realphilosophie,* where Hegel characterizes the experience of pure Self qua "abstract negativity," the "eclipse of (constituted) reality," the contraction into self of the subject, as the "night of the world":

> The human being is this night, this empty nothing, that contains everything in its simplicity – an unending wealth of many representations, images, of which none happens to him – or which are not present. This night, the inner of nature, that exists here – pure self – in phantasmagorical presentations, is night all around it, in which here shoots a bloody head – there another white shape, suddenly here before it, and just so disappears. One catches sight of this night when one looks human beings in the eye – into a night that becomes awful.[7]

And the symbolic order, the universe of the Word, *logos,* can only emerge from the experience of this abyss. As Hegel puts it, this inwardness of the pure self "must enter also into existence, become an object, oppose itself to this innerness to be external; return to being. This is language as name-giving power. . . . Through the name the object as individual entity is born out of the I."[8] What we must be careful not to miss here is how Hegel's break with the Enlightenment tradition can be discerned in the reversal of the very metaphor for the subject: the subject is no longer the Light of Reason opposed to the nontransparent, impenetrable Stuff (of Nature, Tradition . . .); his very kernel, the gesture that opens up the space for the Light of Logos, is absolute negativity qua "night of the world," the point of utter madness in which fantasmatic apparitions of "partial objects" wander around. Consequently, there is no subjectivity without this gesture of withdrawal, which is why Hegel is fully justified in inverting the standard question of how the fall-regression into madness is possible: the true question is rather how the subject is able to climb out of madness and to reach "normalcy." That is to say, the withdrawal into self, the cutting off of the links to the *Umwelt,* is followed by the construction of a symbolic universe that the subject projects onto reality as a kind of substitute-formation destined to recompense us for the loss of the immediate, presymbolic real. However, as Freud himself asserted apropos of Schreber, is not the manufacturing of a substitute-formation that recompenses the subject for the loss of reality the most succinct definition of paranoiac construction as an attempt to cure the subject of the disintegration of his universe? In short, the ontological necessity of "madness" resides in the fact that it is not possible to pass directly from the purely "animal soul" immersed in its natural life-world to "normal" subjectivity dwelling in its symbolic universe – the vanishing mediator between the two is the "mad" gesture of radical withdrawal from reality that opens up the space for its symbolic (re)constitution. It was already Hegel who emphasized the radical ambiguity of the statement "What I think, the product of my thought, is objectively true." This statement is a speculative proposition that renders simultaneously the "lowest truth," the erratic attitude of the madman

9

caught in his self-enclosed universe, unable to relate to reality, *and* the "highest truth," the truth of speculative idealism, the identity of thought and being. If, therefore, in this precise sense, as Lacan put it, normalcy itself is a mode, a subspecies of psychosis, that is, if the difference between "normalcy" and madness is inherent to madness, in what does then this difference between the "mad" (paranoiac) construction and the "normal" (social construction of) reality consist? Is "normalcy" ultimately not merely a more "mediated" form of madness? Or, as Schelling put it, is normal Reason not merely "regulated madness?"

Hegel's notion of the "night of the world" as the feminine kernel of subjectivity is thus profoundly "Schellingian" in that it subverts the simple opposition between the Light of Reason and the impenetrable darkness of matter. Its ultimate consequence is that the emergence of reality, of the universe as such, is grounded in a fundamental and irreducible inversion/perversion of the "proper" relationship between ontological forces – if their relationship were to be "set straight," reality as such would disintegrate. Schelling sticks to this fundamental insight of *Weltalter* up to his late philosophy of mythology and revelation: the universe as such (the actual world) is the result of an original inversion/perversion of divine "potencies": "reality" emerges when the harmonious balance between the three primordial divine potencies (A^1, A^2, A^3) is disturbed, that is, when the first potency (A^1), which should serve as the passive ground for the other, higher potencies, usurps the leading place and thus changes from a benevolent enabling force effective from the background, to an egotist contractive force destructive of every otherness. It is only through this perversion/inversion of potencies that the passage from mere potentiality to actuality can occur – the realm of harmony previous to the perversion of potencies is a realm of pure potentiality that lacks the firmness of actual being. Therein resides the great insight of German Idealism: the real, material world is not merely a (distorted) reflection of suprasensible Ideas in the mode of Plotinus's emanation but involves a violent reversal of the proper hierarchical relation between Ideas. Schelling's name for this reversal is the force of egotism, of contractive Selfsameness (*Ichheit, Selbstheit*) that provides the firm ground of reality: this Selfsameness is neither passive matter nor universal notional content, but the active force of absolute contraction to a point of self-relating that can only occur in the sphere of the Spirit – matter cannot absolutely contract itself into itself, since it has its center of gravity *outside* itself (as is proven by the phenomenon of gravity). In short, Schelling's crucial point is that the domain of Ideas becomes actual Spirit only through its "egotist" perversion/inversion, in the guise of the absolute contraction into a real Person. One must be careful not to miss the point here: it is not only that what we experience as "material reality" is the perversion/inversion of the true ideal order; reality emerges insofar as the true ideal order gets inverted in itself, runs amok – in Schelling's terms, *the inertia of external material reality is a proof of the divine madness, of the fact that God himself was "out of his mind."* (What Schelling is not ready to accept is the logical consequence of his reasoning: this perversion is unsurpassable, the Spirit in its actuality is irreducibly "out of joint," the stain of perversion is the unavoidable price for the Spirit's actualization – the notion of a Reconciliation that would "sublate" the contractive force of egotism in the ethereal medium of Spirit is purely fantasmatic, even when it puts on the technological dress of Virtual Reality and presents itself as the dream of cutting links with our material body and wandering freely in cyberspace.)

This perversion of the "proper" hierarchical relationship between potencies is the key feature of the German Idealist notion of a philosophical "system." Insofar as this perversion is a free act, the most elementary manifestation of freedom, one can see where the standard reproach (a topos from Kierkegaard to Heidegger), according to which the weak point of Schelling's essay on freedom is that it tries to think together what is incompatible (i.e., freedom and system), falls short. "System," in the precise sense of German Idealism, is a totality that is all-encompassing since it includes/contains its own inversion: in a "system," the relationship between A and B, the "higher" and the "lower" principle, is only fully actualized when, within the domain of B, their proper relationship is inverted, that is, A itself is subordinated to B. We can also see in what sense the notion of system is strictly equivalent to the project of conceiving the Absolute "not only as Substance, but also as Subject," as Hegel put it: the principle of subjectivity means that what is originally a subordinate moment of the Absolute can posit itself as its own Center and subordinate to itself its own substantial presuppositions. Or, to put it in more popular terms, the gesture of the subject par excellence is that of wilfully putting at stake the entire substantial content for a capricious meaningless detail: "I want *this,* even if the whole world goes down." Therein resides what Hegel calls the "infinite right of subjectivity": the subject's freedom has to actualize itself *against* Substance, and it can do so only by way of elevating a contingent, meaningless particular moment that the subject posits as its embodiment, over the entire substantial content.

This inclusion of the inversion of the "proper" relationship is not only the key feature of Schelling's notion of freedom (as the freedom for good *and* evil, i.e., the freedom to invert the proper relationship), but also Fichte's and Hegel's, and even Kant's. Is not the aim of Fichte's "doctrine of science" to explain how the subject at the transcendental level, the pure I, which "posits" the entire objective content, experiences itself as passively determined by the universe of objectivity, how the proper relationship between Subject and Object is inverted? Is not the whole point of Hegel's theory of "alienation" to explain how the product of social activity is reified into an autonomous substantial content that subordinates to itself its own generative force? And do we not encounter the same inversion in the fundamental Kantian deadlock that resides in the overlapping of the condition of impossibility (the inaccessibility of the noumenal realm to finite human conscience) with the condition of possibility (humanity can act morally, out of Duty, only insofar as the noumenal realm is inaccessible to human beings) – humanity's limitation to finitude, that is, the very condition that prevents it from ever being able to fulfil its ethical destination, is at the same time a positive condition of its ethical activity? *Subject, freedom,* and *system* are thus three names for the same gesture of inversion.

Jean-Pierre Dupuy[9] developed a homologous notion of autonomous system by way of confronting Derridean deconstruction with the "theory of systems": the latter defines an autonomous system by the very feature that deconstruction denounces as the

index of the system's failure to achieve autonomy, that is, t
fact that the system contains (in both senses of the term: tc
compass and to restrain) its "condition of impossibility," an t
ment that inverts/subverts its fundamental constellation – it was
already Hegel who conceived the Absolute as that which, in its
relation to its Otherness, relates to itself . . . Dupuy conceives
this inherent inversion as the elementary "logical matrix of
deconstruction": in the dominant field I, 2 is subordinated to 1,
whereas in the subordinated field II, 1 itself is subordinated to 2.
In general, Rhetoric is subordinated to Thought (rhetoric should
serve as a mere device to express our thought more clearly); however, within the rhetorical domain itself, Thought is subordinated
to Rhetoric (rhetorical manipulations sooner or later "contami-
nate" thought itself and subordinate it to its goal of achieving a
persuasive "rhetorical effect") . . . It is easy to discern the same
matrix in Hegel's treatment of the touchy subject of the relationship between Religion and State: Religion (God), of course,
stands over the State, but *within the domain of the State,* State
should exert power over Religion; that is, Religion qua social
institution should follow the State's regulations. The insight into
the necessity of this inversion is what distinguishes Reason from
Understanding: according to the stiff rules of Understanding, if
State is subordinated to Religion, this means that theocracy is the
only legitimate form of government. The clergy should act
directly as politically sovereign; every subordination of Religion
to nonreligious State regulations is a depraved compromise (the
position of "religious fundamentalism"). Reason, however, tells
us that Religion truly rules the world precisely by accepting its
own subordinate role within the sphere that is subordinated to
itself. A King can legitimately exert unlimited power over all terrestrial institutions, inclusive of the Church, only insofar as this
power itself is legitimized as grounded in God. One is tempted to
formulate this reversal, which, perhaps, is ideology at its purest,
in the well-known Marxist terms of the difference between the
dominant agency and the agency that determines "in the last instance": God determines everything "in the last instance," yet he
exerts this determining role in the very form of the rule of the
State over every social institution, inclusive of the Church. An-

13

other example is the way Gypsies function in the social perception of Balkan Slavic nations as a carnivalesque inversion of the
"normal" patriarchal universe – the topsy-turvy world of disar-
ranged social and sexual hierarchies (men with breasts, women
with moustaches, etc.). This inversion is, however, *internal* to the
(patriarchal) Order; it serves as its support: it is only through the
supplement of this inversion that the Order is accomplished, fully
actualized, that it becomes *autonomous*. We are dealing here with
a mutual enveloping best illustrated by Escher's two hands drawing each other: "Sacred" is the all-encompassing sea from which
the domain of the Profane has to separate itself, yet once we are
within the Profane, the Sacred itself starts to function as a special
domain *within* the Profane, enclosed by it, that is, as its "super-
structure," its inherent "excess."[10]

DRIVES AND THEIR ROTARY MOTION

How, then, does Schelling succeed in accounting for this inherent
inversion of the Absolute? Perhaps the most appropriate way is
by focusing on the *problem of Beginning,* the crucial problem of
German Idealism – suffice it to recall Hegel's detailed elaboration
of this problem and all its implications in his *Science of Logic.*
Schelling's fundamental thesis is that, to put it bluntly, *the true
Beginning is not at the beginning:* there is something that precedes
the Beginning itself – a rotary motion whose vicious cycle is
broken, in a gesture analogous to the cutting of the Gordian knot,
by the Beginning proper, that is, the primordial act of decision.
The beginning of all beginnings is, of course, the "In the beginning was the Word" from the Gospel according to St. John: prior to
it, there was nothing, that is, the void of divine eternity. According to Schelling, however, "eternity" is not a nondescript bulk – a
lot of things take place in it. Prior to the Word there is the chaotic-
psychotic universe of blind drives, of their rotary motion, of their
undifferentiated pulsating, and the Beginning occurs when the
Word is pronounced that "represses," rejects into the eternal Past,
this self-enclosed circuit of drives. In short, *at the Beginning
proper stands a resolution, an act of decision that, by way of differentiating between past and present, resolves the preceding unbearable
tension of the rotary motion of drives:* the true Beginning is the

passage from the "closed" rotary motion to the "open" progress, from drive to desire, or, in Lacanian terms, from the Real to the Symbolic. The beginning occurs when one "finds the word" that breaks the deadlock, the vicious cycle, of empty and confused ruminations.

In this precise sense, the problem of the Beginning is the problem of "phenomenalization": how does it happen that God pronounces the Word and thereby discloses himself, appears to himself? We must be careful not to miss this crucial point: as with Hegel, the problem is not how to attain the noumenal In-itself beyond phenomena; the true problem is how and why at all does this In-itself split itself from itself, how does it acquire a distance toward itself and thus clear the space in which it can appear (to itself).

How, then, can this phenomenalization of God, this pronunciation of the Word in him that magically, in an unfathomable way, dispells the impenetrable darkness of drives, occur? *It can only occur on condition that the rotary motion of drives that precedes the Beginning is itself not the primordial, unsurpassable fact.* That is to say, the notion of the vortex of drives as the ultimate foundation, the "origin of all things," renders inconceivable the fact of freedom: how can a Word emerge out of this vortex and dominate it, confer on it its shape, "discipline" it? Consequently, this ultimate Ground of reality, the primordial vortex of drives, this Wheel of Fate that sooner or later engulfs and destroys every determinate object, must be preceded by an unfathomable X that in a way yet to be explained "contracts" drives. Is, however, the primordial vortex of drives not the ultimate ground that nothing can precede? Schelling would entirely agree with that, adding only that the point in question is precisely the exact status of this "nothing": prior to *Grund*, there can only be an abyss (*Ungrund*); that is, far from being a mere *nihil privativum,* this "nothing" that precedes Ground stands for the "absolute indifference" qua the abyss of pure Freedom that is not yet the predicate-property of some Subject but rather designates a pure impersonal Willing (*Wollen*) that wills nothing. At the outset of his "prehistory," prior to the Beginning itself, God unavoidably, of blind necessity that characterizes the workings of Fate (according to the first draft

15

of *Weltalter*), "contracts" Being, that is, a firm, impenetrable Ground. (Schelling, of course, plays upon the double meaning of the term *contraction:* to tighten-compress-condense *and* to catch, to be afflicted with, to go down with [an illness]; the primordial Freedom "contracts" Being as a painful burden that ties it down.) Prior to this primordial contraction, to this act of engendering-ejecting one's Ground, God is, as Schelling puts it in an unsurpassed way in the second draft of *Weltalter*, a pure Nothingness that "rejoices in its nonbeing."[11]

God qua pure Freedom that hasn't yet contracted being thus *stricto sensu* doesn't exist. The spontaneous, self-generated "breach of symmetry" (we are tempted to say: the primordial "vacuum fluctuation," which sets in motion the development of the Absolute) is the primordial contraction by means of which God acquires being. This contraction of/into being is necessarily followed by a counterstroke of expansion – why? Let us step back for a moment and reformulate the primordial contraction in terms of the passage from a self-contented Will that wants nothing to an actual Will that effectively wants something. The pure potentiality of the primordial Freedom, this blissful tranquility, this pure enjoyment, of an unassertive, neutral *Will that wants nothing* actualizes itself in the guise of a *Will that actively, effectively, wants this "nothing,"* that is, the annihilation of every positive, determinate content. By means of this purely formal conversion of potentiality into actuality, the blissful peace of primordial Freedom thus changes into pure contraction, into the vortex of "divine madness" that threatens to swallow everything, into the highest affirmation of God's egotism, which tolerates nothing outside itself. In other words, the blissful peace of primordial Freedom and the all-destructive divine fury that sweeps away every determinate content are one and the same thing, only in a different modality: first in the mode of potentiality, then in the mode of actuality: "the same principle carries and holds us in its ineffectiveness that would consume and destroy us in its effectiveness."[12] Upon experiencing itself as negative and destructive, the Will opposes itself to itself in the guise of its own inherent counterpole, the Will that *wants something*, that is, the positive Will to expansion. However, this positive Will's effort to break through the bars of its self-imposed contraction is doomed, since the antagonism of the two Wills, the contractive one and the expansive one, is here *under the dominance, in the power, of contraction.* God, as it were, repeatedly dashes against his own wall: unable to stay within, he follows his urge to break out, yet the more he strives to escape, the more he is caught in his own trap. Perhaps the best metaphor for this rotary motion is a trapped animal who desperately strives to disengage itself from a snare: although every spring only tightens the snare, a blind compulsion leads the animal to make dash after dash, so that it is condemned to an endless repetition of the same gesture. What we have here is Schelling's grandiose "Wagnerian" vision of God in the state of an endless "pleasure in pain," agonizing and struggling with himself, affected by an unbearable anxiety, the vision of a "psychotic," mad God who is absolutely alone, a One who is "all" since he tolerates nothing outside himself – a "wild madness, tearing itself apart."[13] This rotary motion is horrible because it is no longer impersonal: God already exists as One, as the Subject who suffers and endures the antagonism of drives. Schelling provides here a precise definition of anxiety: anxiety arises when a subject experiences simultaneously the impossibility of closing itself up, of withdrawing fully into itself, and the impossibility of opening itself up, of admitting an Otherness, so that it is caught in a vicious cycle of pulsation – every attempt at creation-expansion-externalization collapses back into itself. This God is not yet the Creator, since in creation the being (the contracted reality) of an Otherness is posited that possesses a minimal self-consistency and exists *outside* its Creator – this, however, is what God in the fury of his egotism is not prone to tolerate.

As Schelling emphasizes again and again, this all-destructive divine vortex remains even today the innermost base of all reality: "if we were able to penetrate the exterior of things, we would see that the true stuff of all life and existence is the horrible."[14] In this sense, all reality involves a fundamental antagonism and is therefore destined to fall prey to Divine fury, to disappear in the "orgasm of forces."[15] "Reality" is inherently fragile, the result of a balance between contraction and expansion that can, at any moment, explode into one of the extremes. Hogrebe resorts here to an analogy from cinema: if the projection of a film is to give rise to an "impression of reality" in the spectator, the reel has to run at the proper speed – if it runs too quickly, the movement on the screen gets blurred and we can no longer discern different objects; if it is too slow, we perceive individual pictures and the continuity that accounts for the impression we are watching "real life" gets lost.[16] Therein resides Schelling's fundamental motif: what we experience as "reality" is constituted and maintains itself through a balance between the two antagonist forces, with the ever-present danger that one of the two sides will "crack," run out of control, and thus destroy the "impression of reality." Is not this speculation confirmed by the premise of contemporary cosmology according to which the "reality" of our universe hangs in the balance, that is, hinges on the fragile tension between expansion and gravitation? If the expansion were just a little bit stronger, the universe would "explode," dissipate, no firm, stable object would form; if, on the contrary, gravitation were a little bit stronger, it would long ago have "collapsed," fallen in . . .

What Schelling aims at with his notion of a fragile balance of antagonistic forces is perhaps best exemplified by an interesting experiment by Komar and Melamid, two Russian painters now living in the United States. Recently, they made two paintings, the "best" and the "worst," drawing on an opinion poll they conducted on a representative sample of the American population. The worst painting, of course, was an abstract composition of sharp-edged triangles and squares in bright red and yellow à la Kandinsky, while the best rendered an idyllic scene, all in blue and green, of a clearing, with George Washington taking a walk near the bank of a river running through it and a Bambi-like deer timidly observing him from the wood. The effect of this painting is repulsive and uncanny because it comes too close to the fantasy that underlies our everyday notion of beauty – the "literal," excessively faithful rendering of the fantasy makes it strange.[17] The Schellingian point of this experiment in irony is that in order for us to experience something as part of "reality," it must involve the right mixture of the two extremes. Schelling is thus well aware that every "reality," including our ethical ideals, involves a mixture of the "highest" and "lowest": like a mobile constructed out of our psychic life, even the highest social ideal has to be sustained secretly by the "lowest" motivations. Let us recall an unexpected example: Diana Fuss[18] detected in Freud a tension between the two aspects of homosexual identification. On the one hand, there is homosexual identification in its horrifying aspect (pre-Oedipal oral-anal introjection, swallowing up the partner); on the other hand, there is latent homosexual identification as the cohesive force of society, opposed to the heterosexual link that introduces the element of disturbance, of the individual's gaining a distance, excluding him- or herself from the group of peers. Far from a contradiction, this ambiguity of the notion of homosexual identification is crucial: as in the case of the notion of the Uncanny, the paradox, the "speculative identity" of the opposites, resides in the fact that social cohesion can take place only insofar as it is supported by its radical opposite, the "pre-Oedipal" cannibalistic logic of introjection – the universe of the Catholic Church is guaranteed by the community of believers eating the flesh of Christ (the Eucharist). So the paradox is that the Oedipal couple, far from unambiguously supporting social cohesion, can also undermine it and must therefore be subordinated to the homosexual logic of the group identification of peers.

This logic of presymbolic antagonism, of the rotary motion of drives, is not to be confounded with the *Lebensphilosophie* problematic of the prelogical life substance of "irrational" drives: the status of rotary motion prior to the Beginning is thoroughly logical, since we are dealing with a *failed* logic, with an endlessly repeated effort to begin, that is, to posit the identity-and-difference between the (logical) Subject and Predicate. Prior to the Beginning, there is in a sense only the failed Beginning, failed attempts at the Beginning, that is, a sterile repetition caught in its vicious cycle, a faltering effort that repeatedly collapses back into itself, unable to "take off" properly. As was conclusively demonstrated by Hogrebe, the endless oscillation between contraction and expansion is propelled by the impossibility of formulating the "stable" relationship between S and P that forms the structure of a propositional judgment: the subject (also and above all in the logical sense of the term) "contracts" itself and annihilates its predicative content, whereas in the ensuing gesture of expansion, it passes over into the predicate and thereby loses the firm ground of its self-consistency.

Another confusion to be avoided here is with the common-sense notion (to which, from time to time, all great theoreticians of antagonism succumb, not only Schelling but also Freud in his *Civilization and Its Discontents*, for example) of Eros and Thanatos, or expansion and contraction as two opposed forces engaged in an unrelenting battle for domination. The codependence of the two antagonistic forces does not reside in the fact that one force needs the other as the only ground against which it can assert itself (no light without darkness, no love without hate . . .); much closer is Marx's crucial concept of a "tendency" that can lead to countereffects: the long-term "tendency" of the profit rate to fall, for example, can set in motion the "defense mechanisms" of Capital, which – in the short term, at least – *raise* the profit rate. As was demonstrated by Jacqueline Rose, Melanie Klein's depiction of the presymbolic antagonisms of psychic life involves a homologous mechanism: one and the same cause can bring about opposite effects; that is, it sets in motion a process whose outcome is radically undecidable: excessive aggressivity can be counteracted by a suppression of aggressivity, *or it can trigger the upward spiral of more and more aggressivity.* Homosexuality can arise out of the very anxieties generated by overly strong heterosexual fantasies; anxiety and guilt at times check libidinal development and at other times enhance it (since, as a reaction to anxiety and guilt, the subject is pushed toward the integrative work of restitution). One shouldn't miss the crucial point here: homosexuality does not emerge as the revolt of the suppressed "polymorphous perversity" against the heterosexual phallic economy but *as a reaction to the very excessive strength of heterosexual fantasies.* It was already Freud who, in *The Ego and the Id*, indicated this paradoxical logic when he emphasized that the "progress" of culture is founded upon a libidinal "regression" or regressive fixation. One cannot escape the paradox by recourse to the infamous distinction between the two "aspects" or "levels": the point is not that what, at the level of culture, stands for a form of "progress" is, at the level of biological maturation, a regressive fixation; the problem is that libidinal "progress" itself can take place only as a reaction to an excessively "regressive" libidinal fixation, the same as with a highly developed moral sensitivity, which can emerge only as a reaction to an excessive propensity to Evil. Or, to take a further example from Klein: the very precocious formation of an overdeveloped ego can start to function as an obstacle to its further development, and vice versa.[19] Two characteristics of this paradoxical causality should be retained: a cause is inherently undecidable – it can enhance the feature it stands for or its opposite; and, above all, there is no "proper measure" in the relationship between a cause and its effect – the effect is always in excess of its cause, either in the guise of the upward spiral (aggressivity leads to more and more aggressivity) or in the guise of the counteraction (awareness of aggressivity brings forth a fear of "overreacting" that deprives the subject of the "normal" measure of aggressive self-assertion).

THE UGLY *JOUISSANCE*

This Schellingian problematic also enables us to approach in a new way the status of the "ugly." Contrary to the standard idealist argument that conceives ugliness as the defective mode of beauty, as its distortion, one should assert the *ontological primacy of ugliness*: it is beauty that is a kind of defense against the Ugly in its repulsive existence – or, rather, against existence *tout court,* since, as we shall see, what is ugly is ultimately the brutal fact of existence (of the real) as such.[20]

The ugly object is an object that is in the wrong place, that "shouldn't be there." This does not mean that the ugly object is no longer ugly the moment we relocate it to its proper place; rather, an ugly object is "in itself" out of place, on account of the distorted balance between its "representation" (the symbolic features we perceive) and "existence" – being ugly, out of place, is the excess of existence over representation. Ugliness is thus a *topological* category; it designates an object that is in a way "larger than itself," whose existence is larger than its representation. The ontological presupposition of ugliness is therefore a gap between an object and the space it occupies, or – to make the same point in a different way – between the outside (surface) of an object (captured by its representation) and its inside (formless stuff). In the case of beauty, we have in both cases a perfect isomorphism, while in the case of ugliness, the inside of an object somehow is (appears) larger than the outside of its surface representation (like the uncanny buildings in Kafka's novels that, once we enter them, appear much more voluminous than they seemed from the outside).

Another way to put it is to say that what makes an object "out of place" is that it is too close *to me,* like the statue of Liberty in Hitchcock's *Foreign Correspondent:* seen from extreme proximity, it loses its dignity and acquires disgusting, obscene features. In courtly love, the figure of *die Frau-Welt* obeys the same logic: she appears beautiful from the proper distance, but the moment the poet or the knight serving her approaches too close to her, she turns to him her other, reverse side, and what was previously the semblance of a fascinating beauty is suddenly revealed as putrefied flesh, crawling, snakes and worms, the disgusting substance of life, as in the films of David Lynch where an object turns disgusting when the camera gets too close to it.[21] The gap that separates beauty from ugliness is thus the very gap that separates reality from the Real: the kernel of reality is horror, horror of the Real, and what constitutes reality is the minimum of idealization the subject needs in order to be able to sustain the Real. Another way to make the same point is to define ugliness as the excess of stuff that penetrates through the pores in the surface, from science fiction aliens whose liquid materiality overwhelms their surface (see the evil alien in *Terminator 2* or, of course, the alien from *Alien* itself), to the films of David Lynch where (exemplarily in *Dune*) the raw flesh beneath the surface threatens to emerge. In our standard phenomenological attitude toward the body of another person, we conceive the surface (of a face, for example) as directly expressing the "soul" – we suspend the knowledge of what actually exists beneath the skin surface (glands, flesh . . .). The shock of ugliness occurs when the surface is actually cut, opened up, so that the direct insight into the actual depth of the skinless flesh dispells the spiritual, immaterial pseudodepth.

In the case of beauty, the outside of a thing – its surface – encloses, overcoats, its interior, whereas in the case of ugliness, this proportionality is perturbed by the excess of the interior stuff that threatens to overwhelm and engulf the subject. This opens up the space for the opposite excess, that of something that is not there and should be, like the missing nose that makes the "phantom of the opera" so ugly.[22] Here, we have the case of a lack that also functions as an excess, the excess of a ghostly, spectral materiality in search of a "proper," "real" body. Ghosts and vampires are shadowy forms in desperate search for the life substance (blood) in us, actually existing humans. The excess of stuff is thus strictly correlative to the excess of spectral form: it was already Deleuze who pointed out how the "place without an object" is sustained by an "object lacking its proper place" – it is not possible for the two lacks to cancel each other. What we have here are the two aspects of the real: existence without properties and an object with properties without existence.[23] Suffice it to recall the well-known scene from Terry Gilliam's *Brazil* in which, in a high-class restaurant, the waiter recommends to his customers the best offers from the daily menu ("Today, our tournedo is really special!"), yet what the customers get on making their choice is a dazzling color photo of the meal on a stand above the plate, and on the plate itself, a loathsome excremental lump: this split between the image of the food and the real of its formless remainder exemplifies perfectly the two modes of ugliness, the ghostlike substanceless appearance ("representation without existence") and the raw stuff of the real ("existence without appearance").

One should not underestimate the weight of this gap that separates the "ugly" Real from the fully formed objects in "reality": Lacan's fundamental thesis is that a minimum of "idealization," of the interposition of fantasmatic frame by means of which the subject assumes a distance vis-à-vis the Real, is constitutive of our sense of reality – "reality" occurs insofar as it is not (it does not come) "too close." Today, one likes to evoke our loss of contact with the authentic reality of external (as well as our internal) nature – we are so accustomed to aseptic, pasteurized milk that milk direct from a cow is unpleasant. This "true milk" necessarily strikes us as too dense, disgusting, undrinkable . . .

This, of course, brings us back to Schelling: the gap between the ethereal image and the raw fact of the – inert, dense – Real is precisely the gap between Existence (ethereal form) and its impenetrable Ground, on account of which, as Schelling puts it, the ultimate base of reality is the Horrible. Crucial for any materialist ontology is this gap between the bodily depth of the Real and the pseudodepth of Meaning produced by the Surface. It is also easy to see the connection with Freud, who defined reality as that which functions as an obstacle to desire: "ugliness" ultimately stands for existence itself, for the resistance of reality, which never simply lends itself effortlessly to our molding. Reality is ugly; it "shouldn't be there" and hinder our desire. However, the situation is here more complicated, since this obstacle to desire is at the same time the site of unbearable, filthy, excessive pleasure – of *jouissance*. What shouldn't be there is thus ultimately *jouissance* itself: the inert stuff is the materialization of *jouissance*. In short, the point not to be missed is that, in the opposition between desire and the hard reality (bringing pain, unpleasure, preventing us from achieving the balance of pleasure), *jouissance* is on the side of "hard reality." Jouissance as "real" is that which resists (symbolic integration); it is dense and impenetrable. In this precise sense, *jouissance* is "beyond the pleasure principle." *Jouissance* emerges when the very reality that is the source of unpleasure, of pain, is experienced as a source of traumatic-excessive pleasure. Or, to put it in yet another way: desire is in itself "pure," it endeavors to avoid any "pathological" fixation.[24] The "purity" of desire is guaranteed by its residing in the very gap between any positive object of desire and desire itself. The fundamental experience of desire is *ce n'est pas ça*, this is not that. In clear contrast to it, *jouissance* (or libido, or drive) is by definition "dirty" and/or ugly, it is always "too close": desire is absence, while libido-drive is presence.

All this is absolutely crucial for the functioning of ideology in the case of our "everyday" sexism or racism: their ultimate problem is precisely how to "contain" the threatening inside from "spilling out" and overwhelming us. Are women's periods not the exemplary case of such an ugly inside spilling out? Is the presence of African-Americans not felt as threatening precisely insofar as it is experienced as too massive, too close? Suffice it to recall the racist caricatural cliché of black heads and faces: with eyes bulging out, mouth too-large, as if the outside surface is barely able to contain the inside threatening to break through. (In this sense, the racist fantasmatic duality of blacks and whites coincides with the duality of formless stuff and shadowy-spectral-impotent form without stuff.) Is the concern with how to dispose of shit (which, according to Lacan, is one of the crucial features differentiating human beings from animals) also not a case of how to get rid of the inside that emerges? The ultimate problem in intersubjectivity is precisely the extent to which we are ready to accept the other, our (sexual) partner, in the real of his or her existence – do we still love him when she or he defecates, makes unpleasant sounds? (See the incredible extent to which James Joyce was ready to accept his wife Nora in the "ugly" *jouissance* of her existence.) The problem, of course, is that, in a sense, life itself *is* "ugly": if we truly want to get rid of the ugliness, we are forced to adopt the attitude of a Cathar, for whom terrestrial life is a hell and the God who created this world is Satan himself, the Master of the World. So, in order to survive, we do need a minimum of the real – in a contained, gentrified condition.

The Lacanian proof of the Other's existence is the *jouissance* of the Other (in contrast to Christianity, for example, where this proof is Love). In order to render this notion palpable, suffice it to imagine an intersubjective encounter: when do I effectively encounter the Other "beyond the wall of language," in the real of his or her being? Not when I am able to describe her, not even when I learn her values, dreams, and so on, but only when I encounter the Other in her moment of *jouissance:* when I discern in her a tiny detail – a compulsive gesture, an excessive facial expression, a tic – that signals the intensity of the real of *jouissance.* This encounter of the real is always traumatic, there is something at least minimally obscene about it, I cannot simply integrate it into my universe, there is always a gap separating me from it. This, then, is what "intersubjectivity" is actually about, not the Habermasian "ideal speech situation" of a multitude of academics smoking pipes at a round table and arguing about some point by means of undistorted communication: without the element of the real of *jouissance,* the Other remains ultimately a fiction, a purely symbolic subject of strategic reasoning exemplified in "rational-choice theory." For that reason, one is even tempted to replace the term *multiculturalism* with *multiracism:* multiculturalism suspends the traumatic kernel of the Other, reducing it to an aseptic folklorist entity. What we are dealing with here is – in Lacanese – the distance between S and *a*, between the symbolic features and the unfathomable surplus, the "indivisible remainder" of the real; at a somewhat different level, Walter Benn Michaels made the same point in claiming that

> the accounts of cultural identity that do any cultural work require a racial component. For insofar as our culture remains nothing more than what we do and believe, it is impotently descriptive. . . . It is only if we think that our culture is not whatever beliefs and practices we actually happen to have but is instead the beliefs and practices that should properly go with the sort of people we happen to be that the fact of something belonging to our culture can count as a reason for doing it. But to think this is to appeal to something that must be beyond culture and that cannot be derived from culture precisely because our sense of which culture is properly ours must be derived from it. This has been the function of race. . . . Our sense of culture is characteristically meant to displace race, but . . . culture has turned out to be a way of continuing rather than repudiating racial thought. It is only the appeal to race that makes culture an object of affect and that gives notions like losing our culture, preserving it, stealing someone else's culture, restoring people's culture to them, and so on, their pathos. . . . Race transforms people who learn to do what we do into the thieves of our culture and people who teach us to do what they do into the destroyers of our culture; it makes assimilation into a kind of betrayal and the refusal to assimilate into a form of heroism.[25]

The historicist/culturalist account of ethnic identity, insofar as it functions as performatively binding for the group accounted for and not merely as a distanced ethnological description, thus has to involve "something more," some transcultural "kernel of the real." (The postmodern multiculturalist only displaces this pathos onto the allegedly more "authentic" Other: hearing "The Star-Spangled Banner" gives no thrill, yet what does give a thrill is

listening to some ritual of Native Americans, of African-
Americans. What we are dealing with here is clearly the inverted
form of racism.) Without this kernel, we remain caught in the
vicious cycle of the symbolic performativity that, in an "idealis-
tic" way, retroactively grounds itself. It is Lacan who – in a
Hegelian way – enables us to resolve this deadlock: the kernel of
the real is the retroactive product, the "fallout," of the very process of symbolization. The "Real" is the unfathomable remainder
of the ethnic substance whose predicates are different cultural
features that constitute our identity; in this precise sense, race
relates to culture like real to symbolic. The "Real" is the unfathomable X at stake in our cultural struggles; it is that on account of which, when somebody learns too much of our culture,
he or she "steals" it from us; it is that on account of which, when
somebody shifts allegiance to another culture, he or she "betrays"
us; and so on. Such experiences prove that there must be some X
that is "expressed" in the cultural set of values, attitudes, rituals
that materialize our way of life. What is stolen, betrayed . . . is
always *objet petit a*, the little piece of the Real.[26]

Jacques Ranciere gave a poignant expression to the "bad sur-
prise" that awaits today's postmodern ideologues of the "end of
politics."[27] It is as if we are witnessing the ultimate confirmation
of Freud's thesis, from *Civilization and Its Discontents*: after every
assertion of Eros, Thanatos reasserts itself with a vengeance. At
the very moment when, according to the official ideology, we are
finally leaving behind the "immature" political passions (the re-
gime of the "political": class struggle and other "outdated" divi-
sive antagonisms) for the postideological pragmatic universe of
rational administration and negotiated consensus, for the universe, free of utopian impulses, in which the dispassionate administration of social affairs goes hand in hand with aestheticized
hedonism (the pluralism of "ways of life") – at this very moment,
the foreclosed political is celebrating a triumphant comeback in
its most archaic form of pure, undistilled racist hatred of the
Other that renders the rational, tolerant attitude utterly impo-
tent. In this precise sense, "postmodern" racism is the *symptom* of
multiculturalist late capitalism, bringing to light the inherent
contradiction of the liberal-democratic ideological project. Lib-

Slavoj Žižek

eral "tolerance" condones the folklorist Other deprived of its substance (like the multitude of "ethnic cuisines" in a contemporary megalopolis); however, any "real" Other is instantly denounced for its "fundamentalism," since the kernel of Otherness resides in the regulation of its *jouissance;* that is, the "real Other" is by definition "patriarchal," "violent," never the Other of ethereal wisdom and charming customs. One is tempted to reactualize here the old Marcusean notion of "repressive tolerance," reconceiving it as the tolerance of the Other in its aseptic, benign form, which forecloses the dimension of the Real of the Other's *jouissance.*

Schelling's insistence on the gap that separates forever the Real of drives from its symbolization also allows for a new approach to the crucial question of the relationship between libidinal economy and symbolic sociopolitical attitudes. Within the "poststructuralist" scene, these two extremes are best exemplified by Jean-François Lyotard, for whom all political positions are "libidinally equal," and Deleuze and Guattari, who endeavor to ground the political difference between Left and Right in the difference between paranoid desire and schizophrenic desire. Fredric Jameson's solution "affirms the Utopian character of all collective experience (including that of fascism and the various racisms) but stresses the requirement of an existential choice of solidarity with a specific concrete group: on this nonformalist view, therefore, social solidarity must precede the ethicopolitical choice and cannot be deduced from it."[28] This position of Jameson's is much more delicate than it may appear: it excludes a whole series of standard positions/solutions, from the eternal leftist temptation to directly "ground" political attitudes in different libidinal economies (apart from Deleuze and Guattari, there is, of course, the standard Freudo-Marxist attempt to establish the correlation between capitalism and the so-called anal-compulsive libidinal economy)[29] to "formalist" attempts to derive a concrete political stance directly from some universal formal presuppositions. This sleight of hand, at work in all idealists from Plato to Habermas, renders invisible the "pathological" particularity of a fantasmatic formation as the necessary "vanishing mediator" between the universal notional frame and our concrete sociopolitical atti-

28

tude.[30] Jameson's position involves two seemingly opposite notions: on the one hand, the assertion of what he calls the "Utopian" aspect (or of what we call the fantasmatic kernel that structures enjoyment) in its *neutrality* (or, to use a more fashionable term, *undecidability*) – enjoyment is not in itself "good" or "bad," "progressive" or "reactionary," but a kind of neutral "stuff" appropriated by different sociopolitical attitudes; on the other hand, the assertion that every "universal" ethicopolitical stance is grounded in a particular "pathological" social identification. The merit of Jameson's solution is that it inverts the standard attitude: it is the pathological kernel of enjoyment that is "universal"; it is the "universal" sociopolitical attitude that is grounded in a particular choice.[31]

THE UNCONSCIOUS ACT

The blind rotary motion of God prior to the pronouncement of the Word is not yet temporal. It doesn't occur "in time," since time already presupposes that God has broken free from the closed psychotic cycle. The common expression "from the beginning of time" is to be taken literally: it is the Beginning, the primordial act of decision/resolution, that constitutes time – the "repression" of the rotary motion into the eternal Past establishes the minimal distance between Past and Present that allows for the linear succession of time. One encounters here the first of Schelling's many anti-Platonic "stings": eternity prior to the Word is the timeless rotary motion, the divine madness, that is *beneath* time, "less than time." However, in contrast to those who emphasize Schelling's affinity with Heidegger's assertion of temporality as the ultimate, unsurpassable horizon of Being, it should be said that nowhere is Schelling farther from Heidegger, from his analytics of finitude, than in his conception of the relationship between time and eternity. For Schelling, eternity is not a modality of time; it is rather time itself that is a specific mode (or rather modification) of eternity: Schelling's supreme effort is *to "deduce" time itself from the deadlock of eternity.* The Absolute "opens up time," it "represses" the rotary motion into the past, in order to get rid of the antagonism in its heart that threatens to drag it into the abyss of madness. On the other hand – and, again, in clear contrast to

29

Heidegger – freedom is for Schelling the moment of "eternity in time," the point of groundless decision by means of which a free creature (man) breaks up, suspends, the temporal chain of reasons and, as it were, directly connects with the *Ungrund* of the Absolute. This Schellingian notion of eternity and time, or, to put it in more contemporary terms, of synchrony and diachrony, is therefore to be opposed to the standard notion of time as the finite/distorted reflection of the eternal Order, as well as to the modern notion of eternity as a specific mode of temporality: *eternity itself begets time in order to resolve the deadlock it became entangled in.* For that reason, it is deeply misleading and inadequate to speak about eternity's "fall into time": the "beginning of time" is, on the contrary, a triumphant ascent, the act of decision/ differentiation by means of which the Absolute resolves the agonizing rotary motion of drives and breaks out of its vicious circle into temporal succession.

Schelling's achievement is here a theory of time unique in that it is not formal but qualitative: in contrast to the standard notion of time that conceives the three temporal dimensions as purely formal (the same content, as it were, travels from the past through the present to the future), Schelling provides a minimal qualitative determination of each dimension. The rotary motion of drives *is in itself past:* it was not once present and now past but *is past from the beginning of time.* The split is as such present; that is, the present stands for the moment of division, of the transformation of drive's undifferentiated pulsation into symbolic difference, whereas the future designates the reconciliation to come. The target of Schelling's critique is here not only the formalism of the standard notion of time, but also, perhaps even primarily, the unavowed prerogative of the present involved in it – for Schelling, this prerogative equals the primacy of mechanical necessity over freedom, of actuality over possibility.

Schelling's "materialism" is therefore encapsulated in his persistent claim that one should presuppose an eternally past moment when God himself was at the mercy of the antagonism of matter, without any guarantee that A – the spiritual principle of Light – would eventually prevail over B – the obscure principle of Ground. Since there is nothing outside God, this "crazy God" –

the antagonistic rotary motion of contracted matter – has to beget out of himself a Son, that is, the Word that will resolve the unbearable tension. The undifferentiated pulsation of drives is thus supplanted by the stable network of differences that sustains the self-identity of the differentiated entities: in its most elementary dimension, Word is the medium of differentiation. We encounter here what is perhaps the fundamental conceptual opposition of Schelling's entire philosophical edifice: the opposition between the atemporal "closed" rotary motion of drives and the "open" linear progression of time. The act of "primordial repression" by means of which God ejects the rotary motion of drives into the eternal past and thereby "creates time," that is, opens up the difference between past and present, is *his first deed as a free Subject:* in accomplishing it, he suspends the crippling alternative of the subjectless abyss of Freedom and the Subject who is unfree, caught in the vicious cycle of rotary motion.

This primordial act of "repression" that opens up the dimension of temporality *is itself "eternal," atemporal,* in strict homology to the primordial act of decision by means of which a man chooses his eternal character. That is to say, apropos of Schelling's claim that human consciousness arises from the primordial act that separates the present-actual consciousness from the spectral, shadowy realm of the unconscious, one has to ask a seemingly naive, but crucial question: what, precisely, is here unconscious? Schelling's answer is unambiguous: "unconscious" is not primarily the rotary motion of drives ejected into the eternal past; "unconscious" is rather the very act of *Ent-Scheidung* by means of which drives were ejected into the past. Or, to put it in slightly different terms: what is truly unconscious in man is not the immediate opposite of consciousness, the obscure and confused "irrational" vortex of drives, but the very founding gesture of consciousness, the act of decision by means of which I "choose myself," that is, combine this multitude of drives into the unity of my Self. The "Unconscious" is not the passive stuff of inert drives to be used by the creative "synthetic" activity of the conscious Ego; the "unconscious" in its most radical dimension is rather *the highest Deed of my self-positing,* or, to resort to later "existentialist" terms, the choice of my fundamental "project" that, in order to remain operative, must be "repressed," kept unconscious, out of the light of the day. To quote from the admirable last pages of the second draft of *Weltalter:*

> That primordial deed which makes a man genuinely himself precedes all individual actions; but immediately after it is put into exuberant freedom, this deed sinks into the night of unconsciousness. This is not a deed that could happen once and then stop; it is a permanent deed, a never-ending deed, and consequently it can never again be brought before consciousness. For man to know of this deed, consciousness itself would have to return into nothing, into boundless freedom, and would cease to be consciousness. This deed occurs once and then immediately sinks back into the unfathomable depths; and nature acquires permanence precisely thereby. Likewise that will, posited once at the beginning and then led to the outside, must immediately sink into unconsciousness. Only in this way is a beginning possible, a beginning that does not stop being a beginning, a truly eternal beginning. For here as well, it is true that the beginning cannot know itself. That deed once done, it is done for all eternity. The decision that in some manner is truly to begin must not be brought back to consciousness; it must not be called back, because this would amount to being taken back. If, in making a decision, somebody retains the right to reexamine his choice, he will never make a beginning at all.[32]

What we encounter here is, of course, the logic of the vanishing mediator, of the founding gesture of differentiation that must sink into invisibility once the difference between the "irrational" vortex of drives and the universe of *logos* is in place. This passage from pure Freedom to a free Subject relies on the opposition between being and becoming, between the principle of identity and the principle of (sufficient) reason-ground. Freedom involves the principle of identity; it designates the abyss of an act of decision that breaks up the causal chain, since it is grounded only in itself (when I accomplish a truly free act, I do it for no determinate reason, solely "because I wanted to do it"). Ground designates the existing reality as the network of causes and effects where "nothing happens without a reason-ground." This opposition between identity and ground overlaps with that between eternity and time: when things are conceived in the mode of identity, they appear sub specie aeternitatis, in their absolute contemporaneity, that is, the way they are according to their eternal essence. When they are conceived in the mode of ground, they appear in their temporal becoming, that is, as passing moments of the complex causal network where the past "grounds" the present. In this precise sense, freedom is atemporal: a flash of eternity in time. However, the problem Schelling is struggling with is that Necessity and Freedom are also opposed as atemporal logic and temporal narrative: "Identity" also stands for the Eleatic universe of atemporal logical necessity in which there is no free development, in which everything coexists in absolute contemporaneity, whereas actual freedom is possible only in time, as a contingent-free decision of an actual Entity in its becoming. Schelling's effort is here to think freedom as the atemporal abyss of identity (the miracle of an act that is "its own beginning," grounded only in itself) *and* as the predicate of a free Subject who decides in time. In short, he endeavors to accomplish the passage from Freedom to a free Subject, from the impersonal *Es* of "there is Freedom" to "him," a God who is free. This passage of Freedom from Subject to Predicate involves a reversal that is strictly homologous to the paradigmatic Hegelian reversal of subject and predicate (from "determining reflection" to "reflective determination," etc.): from Freedom's self-limitation/contraction we pass to a self-limited/contracted (i.e., actually existing) Entity that *is free*. Therein resides the ultimate mystery of Schelling's *Weltalter,* as well as of the Hegelian dialectical reversal: freedom is "in itself" a movement of boundless expansion that cannot be constrained to any limited entity – so how can it become the predicate of precisely such a limited entity? Schelling's answer is that Freedom can become the predicate of a Subject only insofar as this Subject accomplishes the act of self-differentiation by means of which it posits itself as grounded in and simultaneously different from its contracted Substance: a free Subject has to have a Ground that is not itself; it has first to contract this Ground and then to assume a free distance toward it via the act of primordial decision that opens up time.

The critical point of *Weltalter* – and, at the same time, the ultimate resort of its breathtaking magnitude, the sign of the absolute

33

integrity of Schelling's thought and the feature on account of which the *Weltalter* fragments are the founding text of dialectical materialism – resides in the repeated failure of Schelling's desperate endeavor to avoid the terrifying intermediate stage between the pure, blissful indifference of the primordial Freedom and God as a free Creator.[33] What comes between the primordial Freedom and God qua free Subject is a stage in which God is already a Subject (he becomes a Subject when, by means of contraction, he acquires reality), but not yet a *free* one. In this stage, after contracting being, God is submitted to the blind necessity of a constricted rotary motion, like an animal caught in the trap of its own making and destined to repeat endlessly the same meaningless motions. The problem is that God's Reason, his awareness of what goes on, in a sense comes too late, is one step behind this blind process, so that later, when he pronounces the Word and thereby attains actual freedom, he can in a sense only acknowledge, accept, what he "contracted" not even unwillingly but in the course of a blindly spontaneous process in which his free Will simply played no part.[34] In other words, the problem is that "one has to admit a moment of blindness, even of 'madness,' in the divine life," on account of which creation appears as "a process in which God was engaged at His own risk, if one may put it this way."[35] In the three consecutive drafts of *Weltalter*, Schelling proposes three different versions of this traumatic moment of "short circuit" between freedom and existence, that is, of the primordial contraction that disturbs the beatitude and peace of pure Freedom, or, in the terms of quantum physics, that breaks the original symmetry:

In the first draft, the primordial Freedom *qua* Will that wants nothing *"contracts" being* – that is, condenses itself into a contracted point of material density – *of necessity*, not through an act of free decision: the primordial contraction cannot not happen, since it derives from primordial Freedom in an absolutely immediate, "blind," nonreflected, unaccountable way. The first inner tension of the Absolute is here the tension between expansive freedom and the blind necessity of contraction.

The second draft, which goes farthest in the direction of Freedom, endeavors to conceive *the primordial contraction itself as a free act:* as soon as the primordial Freedom actualizes itself, as soon as it turns into an actual Will, it splits into two opposed Wills, so that the tension is here strictly internal to freedom; it appears as the tension between the will-to-contraction and the will-to-expansion.

The third draft already delineates the solution adopted by Schelling's late "positive philosophy." In it, Schelling avoids the problem of the passage of freedom to existence by conceiving the starting point of the entire processs, the primordial Freedom, as a "synthetic principle," as the simultaneity of freedom and necessary existence. God is an Entity that exists necessarily; his existence is guaranteed in advance, and *for that very reason* the creation of the universe outside God is a contingent, truly free act, that is, an act that also could not have happened – God is not engaged in it, it is not his own being that is at stake in it. The shift, the displacement, with regard to the first two drafts is here enormous: from a God who is *implicated* in the process of creation, to whom this process is his own Way of the Cross, we pass to a God who creates the universe from a safe distance of "metalanguage."

In a somewhat risky interpretive gesture, one is tempted to assert that the three consecutive drafts of *Weltalter* provide a condensed mirror-reflection of the three main stages of Schelling's entire philosophical development:

Schelling$_1$ (his "philosophy of identity") is in the power (exponent) of Being; that is, in it, necessity encompasses freedom, and freedom can only reside in the "comprehended necessity," in our awareness of the eternal order of rational Necessity in which we participate. In short, Schelling is here a Spinozist for whom the notion of the Absolute involves the absolute contemporaneity, copresence, of its entire content; consequently, the Absolute can only be conceived in the mode of logical deduction that renders its eternal inner articulation – temporal succession is merely an illusion of our finite point of view.

In contrast to it, Schelling$_2$ (of "Philosophical Investigations" and *Weltalter*) is in the power (exponent) of Freedom, which is why his crucial problem is that of "contraction": how did the abyss of primordial Freedom contract Being? Consequently,

35

with regard to the mode of the presentation of the Absolute, logical deduction has to give way to mythical *narrative*.[36]

Finally, the notion of God in Schelling₃ unites freedom and necessary existence, but the price for it is the split of philosophy into "positive" and "negative": negative philosophy provides the a priori deduction of the notional necessity of *what* God and the universe are; however, this *What-ness (Was-Sein)* cannot ever account for the fact *that* there are God and the universe. It is the task of positive philosophy to function as a kind of "transcendental empiricism" and to "test" the truth of rational constructions in actual life.

One is tempted to draw a comparison between, on the one hand, the passage from *Weltalter* to Schelling's late philosophy of mythology, with its dichotomy of positive and negative philosophy, and, on the other hand, within the Frankfurt school, the passage from Adorno and Horkheimer's *Dialectics of Enlightenment* to Habermas: in both cases, we have first a condensed great breakthrough that, however, ends in failure and is then followed by a kind of compromise formation, an immense system elaborated in great detail, yet somewhat flat, with the impetus of the earlier work lost. The late Schelling resolves the impasse of *Weltalter* by taking refuge in the "division of labor" between negative and positive philosophy (negative philosophy deduces the scheme of "potencies" of the Absolute in a purely rational way, whereas its positive counterpart merely "verifies" the truth of this a priori construction on the empirical historical content), the same as with Habermas, who resolves the impasse of *Dialectics of Enlightenment* by taking refuge in the "division of labor" between "interaction" and "work," symbolic communication and productive activity. In short, while *Weltalter* endeavors to narrate directly the history of the Absolute, with no guarantee of its final outcome in an a priori rational scheme, the historical narrative of the late philosophy of mythology merely exemplifies – provides with flesh and blood, as it were – the skeleton of the a priori scheme of divine potencies, as in a kind of unintended imitation of the worst kind of Hegelian rational deduction of empirical content. The problem with late Schelling is thus not that he is a reactionary "irrationalist" (the standard hardline Marxist reproach), but that he is all too "rationalist." The ultimate irony of this homology between Schelling and Habermas, of course, is that Habermas, who (in his excellent article on Schelling in *Theorie und Praxis*) was the first to formulate clearly the "regressive" character of Schelling's late philosophy with regard to *Weltalter,* plays the same "regressive" role in the history of the Frankfurt school.

THE FORCED CHOICE OF SYMBOLIZATION

To recapitulate: the crux, the turning point, in the history of the Absolute is the unconscious act of *Ent-Scheidung,* the resolution that, by way of rejecting the vortex of drives, their "mad dance," into the darkness of the "eternal Past," establishes the universe of temporal "progression" dominated by *logos*-light-desire.[37] Contrary to the commonplace according to which Schelling outlined the consequences of the thorough historicization of the Absolute, Schelling's greatest achievement was to *confine* the domain of history, to trace a line of separation between history (the domain of the Word, *logos*) and the nonhistorical (the rotary motion of drives). Therein resides Schelling's relevance for today's debate on historicism: his notion of the primordial act of decision/differentiation (*Ent-Scheidung*) aims at the gesture that opens up the gap between the inertia of the prehistoric Real and the domain of historicity, of multiple and shifting narrativizations; this act is thus a quasi-transcendental unhistorical condition of possibility and, simultaneously, a condition of the impossibility of historicization. Every "historicization," every symbolization, has to "reenact" this gap, this passage from the Real to history. Apropos of Oedipus, for example, it is easy to play the game of historicization and to demonstrate how the Oedipal constellation is embedded in a specific patriarchal context, and so forth; it requires a far greater effort of thought to discern, in the very historical contingency of Oedipus, one of the reenactments of the gap that opens up the horizon of historicity.

What exactly, then, is the relationship between historicization and the Real as its inherent limit? Freud's distinction between "normal" repression (*Verdraengung*) and the primordial repression (*Ur-Verdrängung*) provides a key to it: the first presupposes the second. That is, for a certain content to be repressed it is not sufficient for it to be pushed away from the domain of Consciousness/Preconscious – it must also be exposed to some attraction from the Unconscious, from the side of the already repressed. One should translate this opposition into topological terms: every part of the repressed content is "historicizable"; that is, it should not be stigmatized into the untouchable taboo, since it can be retranslated back into the system Cs/Pcs – everything *except the very form of the Unconscious,* except the empty *place itself* that collects the repressed content. This empty place is created by the primordial repression that relates to "normal" repression as a kind of transcendental, a priori frame to its empirical, a posteriori content. This gesture of "primordial repression," of evacuating the place of the Thing, whose psychoanalytic name is *death drive,* cannot be historicized, since it is the nonhistorical condition of historicity itself. For that reason, *death drive* does not designate the positive content one should directly refer to in order to explain some event ("people kill each other in wars because of the death drive"), but the empty frame within which the game of historicization is taking place: it maintains open the minimal gap, the delay, between an event and the modes of its historicization, of its symbolic inscription; *death drive* stands for the fact that the passage from an event to its historicization is radically contingent, never grounded in the Real itself. (In a similar vein, Derrida speaks of the nondeconstructible conditions of deconstruction.)[38]

How is the emergence of Word connected with the pulsating "rotation" in God, that is, with the interchange of expansion and contraction, of externalization and internalization? How, precisely, does the Word discharge the tension of the rotary motion, how does it mediate the antagonism between the contractive and the expansive force? The Word is a *contraction in the guise of its very opposite, of an expansion;* that is, in pronouncing a word, the subject contracts his being *outside* himself, he "coagulates" the core of his being in an external *sign.* In the (verbal) sign I *find myself outside myself,* as it were; I posit my unity outside myself, in a signifier that represents me: "It seems universal that every creature that cannot contain itself or draw itself together in its own fullness, draws itself together outside itself, whence, e.g., the

elevated miracle of the formation of the word in the mouth belongs, which is a true creation of the full inside when it can no
longer remain in itself."[39] This notion of symbolization (of the
pronunciation of Word) as the contraction of the subject outside
itself, that is, in the form of its very opposite (of expansion),
announces the structural/differential notion of the signifier as an
element whose identity stands for its very opposite (for pure
difference): we enter the symbolic order the moment a feature
functions as the index of its opposite (the moment the political
Leader's hatred – of the "enemies" – is perceived by his subjects as
the very form of appearance of his unlimited love for the People;
the moment the apathetic indifference of a femme fatale is perceived by her male admirers as the token of her intense passion;
etc.). For the very same reason, phallus is for Lacan the "pure"
signifier: it stands for its own opposite. That is, it functions as the
signifier of *castration.* The transition from the Real to the Symbolic, from the realm of presymbolic antagonism (of contraction
and expansion) to the symbolic order in which the network of
signifiers is correlated to the field of meaning, can take place only
by means of a paradoxical "pure" signifier, a signifier without
signified: in order for the field of meaning to emerge, that is, in
order for the series of signifiers to signify *something* (to have a
determinate meaning), *there must be a signifier (a "something")
that stands for "nothing,"* a signifying element whose very presence stands for the absence of meaning (or, rather, for absence
tout court). This "nothing," of course, is *the subject itself,* the subject qua $ (the Lacanian matheme, designating the subject with
all content removed), the empty set, the void that emerges as the
result of the contraction in the form of expansion: when I contract myself outside myself, I deprive myself of my substantial
content. The formation of the Word is thus the exact opposite of
the primordial contraction/abjection by means of which, according to Schelling's *Stuttgart Seminars* from the same time,[40] God
expels – discharges, casts out, rejects out of himself – his real side,
the vortex of drives, and thus constitutes himself in his Ideality, as
a free subject: the primordial rejection is an act of supreme egotism, since in it, God as it were "gets rid of the shit in himself" in
order to purify and keep for himself the precious spiritual essence

39

of his being, whereas in the formation of the Word, he articulates outside himself, that is, he discloses, (sur)renders, this very ideal-spiritual essence of his being. In this precise sense, the formation of the Word is the supreme act and the paradigmatic case of *creation:* "creation" means that I reveal, hand over to the Other, the innermost essence of my being.

The problem, of course, is that this second contraction, this original act of creation, this "drawing together outside itself," is ultimately always unfitting, contingent – it "betrays" the subject, it represents him inadequately. Here, Schelling already announces the Lacanian problematic of a *vel,* of a forced choice that is constitutive of the emergence of the subject: the subject either persists in himself, in his purity, and thereby loses himself in empty expansion, or he gets out of himself, externalizes himself, by way of "contracting" or "putting on" a signifying feature, and thereby alienates himself, that is, is no longer what he is, the void of pure $:

> . . . the subject can never grasp itself *as* what it is, for precisely in attracting itself *[sich-Anziehen]* it *becomes* an other; this is the basic contradiction, we can say the misfortune in all being – for either it *leaves* itself, then it is as nothing, or it attracts-contracts itself, then it is an other and not identical with itself. No longer uninhibited by being as before, but that which has inhibited itself with being, it itself feels this being as alien *[zugezogenes]* and thus contingent.[41]

Therein resides Schelling's reformulation of the classical question "why is there something and not nothing": in the primordial *vel,* the subject has to decide between "nothing" (the unground/abyss of freedom that lacks all objective being, pure $) and "something," but always irreducibly in the sense of "something extra, something additional, something foreign / put on, in a certain respect something contingent."[42] The dilemma is therefore the following: "either it remains still (remains *as* it is, thus pure subject), then there is no life and it is itself as nothing, or it *wants* itself, then it becomes an other, something not the same as itself, *sui dissimile.* It admittedly wants itself *as* such, but precisely this is impossible in an *immediate* way; in the very wanting itself it already becomes an other and distorts itself."[43] Everything thus turns around the primordial act by means of which "nothing" becomes "something," and Schelling's entire philosophical revolution is contained in the assertion that this act that precedes and grounds every necessity is in itself *radically contingent* – for that very reason, it cannot be deduced, inferred, but only retroactively presupposed. This act involves a primordial, radical, and irreducible *alienation,* a distortion of the original balance, a constitutive "out-of-jointedness": "This whole construction therefore begins with the emergence of the first contingency – which is not identical with itself – it begins with a *dissonance,* and *must* begin this way."[44] In order to emphasize the nonspontaneous, "artificial," "corrupted" character of this act, Schelling plays on the multiple meanings of the German verb *Anziehen:* being attracted, drawn to something; contracting a disease; putting on some clothing; acting in a false, pretentious way. Apropos of this last feature, Schelling directly evokes what was later (by Jon Elster)[45] conceptualized as "states which are essentially by-products":

> There are certain moral and other qualities that one only has precisely to the extent that one does not have them, as the German language splendidly expresses it to the extent to which one does not put on *[sich anzieht]* those qualities. E.g., true charm is only possible precisely if it does not know about itself, whereas a person who knows of his charm, who puts it on, immediately stops being charming, and if he conducts himself *as* being charming will instead become the opposite.[46]

The implications of this are very radical and far-reaching: every positive feature, every "something" that we are, is ultimately "put on" – in short, *fake is original.* At this point, one is used to opposing Schelling to Hegel, that is, to the Hegelian logical necessity of the immanent self-deployment of the absolute Idea. Before yielding to this commonplace, however, it would be worth pausing to consider the fact that Hegel develops a homologous *vel* in his *Phenomenology of Spirit,* apropos of the Beautiful Soul and the act. The choice that confronts the subject here is between inactivity and an act that is by definition contingent, branded with a merely subjective content. This contingency of the act disturbs the balance of the (social) Substance in which the subject is embedded;

the reaction of the Substance thereby set in motion inexorably leads to the failure of the subject's enterprise. The true critical "materialist" supplement to Schelling is to be sought elsewhere: in Marx, who, in his dialectics of the commodity form, also starts from the need of the abstract universal Value to embody itself in a contingent use-value, to "put on" a use-value dress, to appear in the form of a use-value; however, as he is quick to add, *at least two* use-values (commodities) are needed if a Value is to express itself, so that the use-value of the first commodity gives body to the Value of the second commodity. And Lacan's definition of the signifier as that which "represents the subject for another signifier" ultimately amounts to the same assertion of an irreducible duality: if a subject is to be represented by a signifier, there must be a minimal chain of two signifiers, one of which represents the subject for the other.

The crucial point not to be missed here is that, insofar as we are dealing with *Subject,* the "contraction" in question is no longer the primordial contraction by means of which the original Freedom catches being and thereby gets caught in the rotary motion of contraction and expansion, but the contraction of the subject outside himself, in an external sign, which resolves the tension, the "inner dispute," of contraction and expansion. The paradox of the Word is therefore that its emergence resolves the tension of the presymbolic antagonism, but at a price: the Word, the contraction of the Self outside the Self, involves an irretrievable externalization-alienation. With the emergence of the Word, we pass from *antagonism* to the Hegelian *contradiction* between $ and S_1, between the subject and its inadequate symbolic representation. This "contingency" of the contraction in the Word points toward what, in the good old structuralist terms, is called "the arbitrariness of the signifier": Schelling asserts the irreducible gap between the subject and a signifier the subject has to "contract" if the subject is to acquire (symbolic) existence: the subject qua $ is never adequately represented in a signifier. This "contradiction" between the subject and a (necessarily, constitutively inadequate) symbolic representation provides the context for Schelling's "Lacanian" formulation according to which God-Absolute *becomes inexpressible at the very moment he expresses himself,* that is, *pronounces a Word.* Prior to his or her symbolic externalization, the subject cannot be said to be "inexpressible" since the medium of expression itself is not yet given, or, to invoke Lacan's precise formulation, desire is *nonarticulable* precisely as always-already *articulated* in a signifying chain. In this precise sense, "subject is not substance": it has no substantial positive being "in itself"; that is, it is caught between "not yet" and "no longer." In other words, the subject never "is," it "will have been" – either the subject is *not yet* here, we still have a presubjective bliss, or it is *no longer* here, since there is only a trace of its absence . . .

In short, by means of the Word, the subject finally *finds* itself, comes to itself: it is no longer a mere obscure longing for itself, since, in the Word, the subject directly attains itself, posits itself as such. The price for it, however, is the irretrievable *loss* of the subject's self-identity: the verbal sign that stands for the subject, that is, in which the subject posits itself as self-identical, bears the mark of an irreducible dissonance; it never "fits" the subject. This paradoxical necessity on account of which the act of returning to oneself, of finding oneself, immediately, in its very actualization, assumes the form of its opposite, of the radical loss of one's self-identity, displays the structure of what Lacan calls "symbolic castration." This castration involved in the passage to the Word can also be formulated as the redoubling, the splitting, of an element into itself and its place in the structure. Apropos of the Word, Schelling refers to the Medieval logic in which *reduplicatio* designated the operation by means of which a term is no longer conceived *simpliciter* but is posited *as such: reduplicatio* points towards the minimal, constitutive gap that forever separates an element from its re-marking in the symbolic network. Hogrebe invokes here the difference between an element and its place *(Platz)* in an anonymous structure.[47] Because of this structure of castration, Spirit is supernatural or extranatural, although it grew out of nature: Nature has an ineradicable tendency to "speak itself out," it is caught in the search for a Speaker *(die Suche nach dem Sprecher)* whose Word would posit it as such; this Speaker, however, can only be an entity that is itself not natural, not part of nature, but Nature's Other. Or, to put it in a slightly different way, Nature is searching for itself, it strives for itself, but it can only "find itself," attain itself, *outside itself*, in a medium that is itself not natural. The moment Nature becomes *ein Aussprechliches* (something that can be spoken of in meaningful propositions), it ceases to be the *Aussprechendes* (that which is speaking):[48] the speaking agency is the Spirit qua $, the substanceless void of non-Nature, the distance of Nature toward itself. In short, the fundamental paradox of symbolization – the paradox the term *symbolic castration* aims at recapturing – is that Nature can attain itself, its self-identity, only at the price of radical decentrement: it can only find itself in a medium outside itself. A father becomes father "as such," the bearer of symbolic authority, only insofar as he assumes his "castration," the difference between himself in the immediate reality of his being and the place in the symbolic structure that guarantees his authority: the father's authority is radically "decentred" with regard to father qua flesh-and-blood person; that is, it is the anonymous structure of the symbolic Law that speaks through him.

Incidentally, the first philosopher to focus on the uncanny contingency in the very heart of subjectivity was none other than Schelling's predecessor and (later) opponent, Fichte: the Fichtean subject is not the overblown Ego = Ego as the absolute Origin of all reality, but a finite subject thrown, caught, in a contingent social situation that forever eludes its mastery. Crucial here is the notion of *Anstoss*, of the primordial impulse that sets in motion the gradual self-limitation and self-determination of the initially void subject.[49] Furthermore, *Anstoss* is not merely a mechanical external impulse: it also points toward another subject who, in the abyss of its freedom, functions as the challenge (*Aufforderung*) compelling me to limit/specify my freedom, that is, to accomplish the passage from the abstract egotist freedom to concrete freedom within the rational ethical universe. Perhaps this intersubjective *Aufforderung* is not merely the secondary specification of the *Anstoss*, but its exemplary original case. It is important to bear in mind the two main meanings of *Anstoss* in German: check, obstacle, hindrance, something that *resists* the boundless expansion of our striving, *and* an impetus, stimulus, something that incites our activity. *Anstoss* is not simply the obstacle the absolute I posits to itself in order to stimulate its activity, so that, by way of overcoming the self-posited obstacle, it asserts its creative power, like the games the proverbial perverted ascetic saint plays with himself by way of inventing ever new temptations and then, in successfully resisting them, confirming his strength. If the Kantian *Ding an sich* corresponds to the Freudian-Lacanian Thing, *Anstoss* is closer to *objet petit a,* to the primordial foreign body that "sticks in the throat" of the subject, to the object – cause of desire that *splits it up:* Fichte himself defines *Anstoss* as the nonassimilable foreign body that causes the subject's division into the empty absolute subject and the finite determinate subject, limited by the non-I. *Anstoss* thus designates the moment of the "run-in," the hazardous knock, the *encounter* of the Real in the midst of the ideality of the absolute I: there is no subject without *Anstoss,* without the collision with an element of irreducible facticity and contingency – "the I is supposed to encounter *within itself* something foreign." The point is thus to acknowledge "the presence, within the I itself, of a realm of irreducible otherness, of absolute contingency and incomprehensibility. . . . Ultimately, not just Angelus Silesius' rose, but every *Anstoss* whatsoever *ist ohne Warum.*"[50] In clear contrast to the Kantian noumenal *Ding* that affects our senses, *Anstoss* does not come from outside, it is *stricto sensu ex-timate:* a nonassimilable foreign body in the very kernel of the subject. As Fichte himself emphasizes, the paradox of *Anstoss* resides in the fact that it is simultaneously "purely subjective" *and* not produced by the activity of the I. If *Anstoss* were not "purely subjective," if it were already the non-I, part of objectivity, we would fall back into "dogmaticism," that is, *Anstoss* would effectively amount to no more than a shadowy remainder of the Kantian *Ding an sich* and would thus bear witness to Fichte's inconsequentiality (the commonplace reproach to Fichte); if *Anstoss* were simply subjective, it would present a case of the hollow playing of the subject with itself, and we would never reach the level of objective reality; that is, Fichte would be effectively a solipsist (another commonplace reproach to his philosophy). The crucial point is that *Anstoss* sets in motion the constitution of "reality": at the beginning is the pure I with the nonassimilable foreign body in its heart, and the subject constitutes reality by way of assuming a distance toward the Real of the formless *Anstoss* and conferring on it the structure of objectivity.[51]

However, Schelling is far from simply providing a new version of the "sublation" of bodily reality in the spiritual medium of the Word; Schelling gives to this "sublation" an uncanny *materialist* twist. The point of his critique of pure spiritual idealism, of its lifeless "negative" nihilism, is that *there is no spirit without spirits-ghosts*, no "pure" spirituality without the obscene specter of "spiritualized matter." In the dialogue *Clara,* from 1810, Schelling drove a wedge into the simple complementary mirror-relationship of Inside and Outside, between Spirit and Body, between the ideal and the real element that together form the living totality of the Organism, by way of calling attention to the double surplus that "sticks out." On the one hand, there is the *spiritual element of corporeality:* the presence, in the matter itself, of a nonmaterial but physical element, of a subtle corpse, relatively independent of time and space, that provides the material base of our free will (animal magnetism, etc.); on the other hand, there is the *corporeal element of spirituality:* the materializations of the spirit in a kind of pseudostuff, in substanceless apparitions (ghosts, living dead). Schelling thus asserts the impossibility of a pure dual relationship between Spirit and body: if Spirit is to acquire its autonomy with regard to body, it has to rely on *another* body, the "undead" body made of ethereal stuff, which lacks proper substantial density and, when we approach it too closely and attempt to seize it directly, disintegrates like the body of a vampire when properly pierced by a wooden stake. There is no Spirit without "undead" spirits-ghosts: the "undead" spectral body always serves as the "material basis" for the immortality of the soul.[52] Modern art provides perhaps the most pertinent case of this spectral materiality. When exemplary modernist artists speak about the Spiritual in painting (Kandinsky) or in music (Schoenberg), the "spiritual" dimension they evoke points toward the "spiritualization" (or, rather, "spectralization") of Matter (color and shape, sound) as such, *outside* its reference to Meaning. Suffice it to recall the "massiveness" of the protracted stains that "are" yellow sky in late

46

van Gogh, or the water or grass in Munch: this uncanny "massiveness" pertains neither to the direct materiality of the color stains nor to the materiality of the depicted objects – it dwells in a kind of intermediate spectral domain of what Schelling called *geistige Koerperlichkeit*. From the Lacanian perspective, it is easy to identify this "spiritual corporeality" as materialized *jouissance, "jouissance* that turned into flesh."[53] In music, we encounter the same "spiritual corporeality" in the Vienna school, in what Webern referred to as *Strukturklang,* the sound of the structure itself, in its opposition to mere *Klangstruktur,* the structure of the sound. The shift from *Klangstruktur* to *Strukturklang* is the shift from the sound that follows the (imposed) tonal structure to an unheard-of sound that is directly the "sound of the structure itself" in its spectral materiality, beyond the sound as the bearer of meaning. This is what "modern music" is really about: the suspension of tonality renders palpable the presence of sounds in the real of their spectral materiality.

There is yet another way to connect Schelling with the modernist break in art. Where does musical modernism proper begin? Perhaps the most reliable way to draw the line of separation is to stick to the surface: at a concert of classical music, the end of a movement is as a rule followed by a sudden outburst of coughing and clearing of throats. There is nothing "natural" in these sounds, they are not a giving way to a long-withheld expression of a bodily need (since, while the music goes on, one must remain silent): they rather bear witness to a kind of metaphysical *horror vacui,* to a compulsion to fill the unbearable silence that confronts the public the moment music is over. In short, these raw chaotic sounds of the public are a strange "prolongation of the music by other means." And, at the most elementary level, one can say that, after a movement of a modernist work, there is no coughing and clearing of one's throat – why? The premodernist piece ends up in a triumphant dissolution of the dissonant tension (exemplarily in the great Wagnerian finales – of *Tristan,* of *Parsifal*); what is properly unbearable and has to be filled by coughing is the silence that follows this "orgasm of forces," as Schelling would have put it, this orgasmic trance, a kind of "subjective destitution" in which the very tension that keeps the subject alive is annihilated. Since, however, a modernist piece does *not* dissolve the dissonant tension, the silence that confronts us at its end is of an entirely different nature: it is no longer the "postcoital" silence that follows the quenched desire, but rather the silence that marks the very absence, or failure, of the proper dissolution.[54]

How does this Schellingian subversion of idealism, his emphasis on the unsurpassable real ground of the universal ideal notion, affect the status of the Universal? It enables him to anticipate the Marxist critique of ideology. That is to say, Schelling was the first to articulate the notion of a "false universal," of a universal beneath which one should discern the umbilical chord that links it to a particular content. It is in this "unmasking" of the false universality (say, in discerning, beneath the universal "rights of Man," the rights of white males) that resides the elementary procedure of the critique of ideology. Schelling's notion of the State as the imposed, "mechanical," unity of society that simultaneously *dissimulates* and *supplements for* the loss of the "organic" social unity clearly announces the Marxist critique of the State as the "alienated" form of social unity. However, the conclusion to be drawn from this is not that every Universal is simply false, subordinated to a Particular: everything in a universal notion is derived from a particular content – *everything except the very empty screen, frame, blank of universality that as it were waits to be filled out with particular content.* In other words, what a critique of ideology has to perform is not a simple reduction of the Universal to a contingent particular content beneath it, but to render visible the gap that forever separates the Universal qua empty frame from the particular content that fills it out, that is, to assert the Universal as the "empty signifier," the battleground for the hegemonic struggle to occupy its void.[55] There is no \$, subject, without the empty signifier: there is a subject-effect the moment the individual is caught in the split between the empty Universal (S_1) and the series of positive features (S_2), that is, in the hegemonic fight for the content of the empty Master Signifier (*nation, black dignity, democracy, ecology . . .*). And one of the most elementary definitions of ideology, of ideological misrecognition, is that it resides in the (mis)perception of the empty Master Signifier as full, in the disavowal of its empty character. We are in ideology the moment we "naturalize" the link between Master Signifier and a set of positive features that define it as the result of a struggle. In this precise sense, the subject is a nonideological concept; that is, subject and subjectivization are to be opposed: we "subjectivize" ourselves when we recognize ourselves in a determinate content of the Master Signifier, in the latter's fullness, whereas the subject is the void correlative to the empty signifier.

The conclusion to be drawn from Schelling's subversion of idealism is thus a paradoxical reassertion of universality: we have access to the Universal, the dimension of the Universal emerges, *because* of our irreducible embeddedness in the context of our particular life-world. That is to say, one might think that, since we are caught in our particular culture and thus cannot ever grasp other cultures in their specific Otherness, every universal notion at our disposal is colored by the implicit assumptions of our predominant horizon of preunderstanding ("human rights" are the rights of a white middle-class male, etc.). What is wrong with this notion is the underlying, apparently self-evident assumption that, in order to communicate with another culture, we have to share some common ideas ("cultural universals") beyond that which divides us. The moment we concede this, we "regress" from the properly Hegelian notion of the dialectical antagonism itself as the aspect that keeps together a totality (the "totalizing" moment of a class society, for example, is not some set of commonly shared features that individuals possess beyond class divisions, but the class struggle itself) to the Habermasian notion of pragmatic-transcendental universals; that is, we lose the properly dialectical paradox according to which "contradiction" ("struggle") unifies, whereas shared "neutral" universals involve only indifferent coexistence. Or, to put it in another way, what makes "communication" between different cultures possible is the fact that the limit that prevents our full access to the Other is *ontological*, not merely epistemological. The epistemological status of this limit leads to a simple historicist relativism: on account of my biased horizon of understanding, the full context of the Other that would enable me really to understand the specificity of the Other's culture forever eludes me; if, however, we conceive of this

limit as ontological, this means that the Other (say, another culture I am trying to understand) is already "in itself" not fully
determined by its context but "open," "floating." To make this
point somewhat clearer, let us imagine the elementary example of
trying to understand a word or a phrase of some foreign language:
we really understand it only when we perceive how our effort to
determine exhaustively its meaning fails not because of the lack
of our understanding but because the meaning of this word is
incomplete already "in itself" (in the Other language). Every language, by definition, contains an aspect of openness to enigma, to
what eludes its grasp, to the dimension in which "words fail."
This minimal openness of the meaning of its words and propositions is what makes a language "alive." We effectively "understand" a foreign culture when we are able to identify with its point
of failure: when we are able to discern not its hidden positive
meaning, but rather its blind spot, the deadlock the proliferation
of meaning endeavors to cover up. In other words, when we endeavor to understand the Other (another culture), we should not
focus on its specificity (on the peculiarity of "their customs,"
etc.); we should rather endeavor to encircle that which eludes
their grasp, the point at which the Other is in itself dislocated, not
bound by its "specific context." The lesson of the well-known
(though discredited) story about the origins of the term *kangaroo*
still holds: the white explorers pointed at a kangaroo and asked
the natives "What is this?" When the natives answered "kangaroo," the explorers thought this was their name for the animal;
later, when they learned the native language, it became clear that
the word *kangaroo* means simply "What do you want?"

The properly Hegelian paradox thus resides in the fact that, far
from preventing "communication" between cultures, this *redoubling* of the limit effectively renders it possible. "The enigmas of
the ancient Egyptians were also enigmas for the Egyptians themselves," as Hegel put it: I understand the Other when I become
aware of how the very problem that was bothering me (the nature
of the Other's secret) is already bothering the Other itself. The
dimension of the Universal thus emerges when the two lacks –
mine and that of the Other – overlap. In other words, the paradox
of the Universal is that its condition of impossibility is its condi-

tion of possibility: the dimension of the Universal emerges precisely and only insofar as the Other is not accessible to us in its
specificity; or, to put it in Lacanian terms: there is no universality
without an *empty signifier*. What we and the inaccessible Other
share is the empty signifier that stands for that X which eludes
both positions. Apropos of "human rights," for example, it is easy
to play the game of historicist reductionism and to prove how the
universality of "human rights" is never neutral, since its specific
content is always overdetermined by a particular historical constellation. The problem, however, is that "human rights" always
function also as an "empty signifier": one can never fully enumer-
ate them; that is, it is part of the very notion of human rights that
they are never "complete," that there are always new (positive)
rights to be added to the list – and the awareness of this "openness" is what enables us and individuals belonging to another
culture to engage in communication and, perhaps, arrive at a
common point by acknowledging the limitation of one's own
position. In Kierkegaardian terms, one has to distinguish the already established Universal from the "Universal-in-becoming":
the Universal in its established "being" is mute universality, the
positive features a multitude of particular situations or objects
have in common, whereas the Universal-in-becoming is the
breach, the "opening," which prevents me from fully identifying
with my own particular situation, that is, which compels me to
take into account the way I am always "out of joint," displaced
with regard to the particular context of my life-world.[56]

Another aspect of this same paradox concerns the notion of
identification.[57] When a (collective or individual) subject "identifies" with an object in the strict Freudian sense of the term, this
in no way involves a pacifying "reconciliation" with the object, a
passive "accommodation" of the subject to the object with which
it identifies; "identification" is, on the contrary, a violent act that
splits the object from within, disturbing its balance, wresting it
from its context and privileging the aspect of the object that starts
to function, via the act of identification, as the placeholder of the
lack/subject (in order to designate this aspect, Lacan uses the
Freudian term *der einzige Zug, le trait unaire,* the "unary feature").
Say, when I identify with a hero figure, I privilege in him a certain

partial feature, thereby reducing the person of the hero to a kind of appendix to this feature (Lacan evokes ironically the small moustache as Hitler's *trait unaire*). At the level of political order, this brings us to the crucial distinction between order and its "ordering" (elaborated by Laclau). Suffice it to recall the recent confused situation in post-Communist Russia, where the main "spontaneous" social demand is a demand for law and order: the winner will be the political party perceived as being able, *irrespective of its concrete political program,* to establish law and order; those opposing *this* party with its concrete program will be perceived as opposing the reestablishment of law and order *as such.* Or, to take another example from the West, the African-American "Million Men March" in Washington on October 16, 1995, organized by Louis Farrakhan's antifeminist and fundamentalist Nation of Islam: Farrakhan succeeded in cornering the more liberal-minded African-Americans. They had to participate since, in that concrete situation, any opposition to Farrakhan was equivalent to the opposition to African-American dignity and self-respect *as such;* the desperate attempts to justify one's participation by emphasizing the distinction between the appalling "messenger" (Farrakhan) and the acceptable "message" was a mere fig leaf concealing the liberals' defeat. Therein, in this inevitable, although always temporary and contingent, short circuit between the (universal) ordering function – in this case, the motif of African-American dignity and self-respect – and the (particular) order – Nation of Islam's fundamentalism – resides the "violence" of identification. What is at stake in the struggle for identification between different positions (liberal, fundamentalist, socialist) is which of these positions will succeed in exerting ideological hegemony, in functioning as the stand-in for (placeholder of) the universal dimension, so that identification with this particular position will "automatically" signify identification with the universality. The multitude of positions (liberal, fundamentalist, socialist) never meets in a neutral space; that is, one can never simply say that African-American liberals, religious fundamentalists, socialists, and so on, each render their own version of (or contribution to) African-American dignity: one can never occupy a neutral place and measure the contribution of each particular position to the African-American cause. In this precise sense, political identification always involves the act of violent splitting, of disturbing the balance by way of privileging one particular position as the immediate stand-in for the universal dimension.

As Ernesto Laclau would have put it, the Universal is simultaneously *necessary* (unavoidable) and *impossible;* necessary, since (as we know at least from Hegel) the symbolic medium as such is universal, and impossible, since the positive content of the Universal is never purely neutral but is always (mis)appropriated, elevated, from some particular content that "hegemonizes" the Universal. Ecology, for example, is never simply a neutral genus of its species – "deep," conservative, feminist, socialist, statist . . . ecology – since, in every concrete situation, ecology "as such" *means* (is contaminated by) some particular content. And it is already here, at this general level, that we encounter the subject: the subject is that X which accomplishes the act of "suture," of connecting the Universal to a particular content, which violently "destabilizes," "throws out of balance," the "objective" order of things. The Lacanian name for such an entity that is simultaneously necessary *and* impossible is, of course, the Real; this same paradox of the Real is at work also in "free associations" within the psychoanalytic cure (we never really have them, one never can fully suspend the pressure of inhibitions and "let oneself go"; at the same time, *whatever one says* on the analytic couch *is* a free association, even if it was carefully planned in advance or is a long line of strict logical reasoning) and in *jouissance: jouissance* eludes us, it is beyond our reach, its full confrontation is lethal; at the same time, however, one can never get rid of it, its remainder sticks to whatever we do. Along the same lines, the Kantian ethical injunction also has the status of a Real: it is impossible fully to realize one's ethical duty, yet it is also impossible to avoid the pressure of the call of duty.[58]

This same gap between the ordering principle and the series of features that define a concrete-positive order – in Lacanian terms, between S_1 (the Master Signifier) and S_2 (the chain of knowledge) – enables us to clarify the way the phallic signifier sustains our capacity to act.[59] Phallus, as the signifier of castration, stands for the gap between the structural principle as such and the person embodying it, functioning as its stand-in. Hamlet is unable to act (to kill Claudius) as long as he identifies Claudius directly with the Name of the Father, the phallic signifier, the agency of symbolic authority; it is only after he distinguishes between the two and becomes aware that Claudius is a mere replaceable stand-in, a substitute, for the Phallus that he is able to finish Claudius off without involving the collapse of his entire universe. Or, again, in Laclau's terms of the difference between ordering and order: as long as the ordering principle, the possibility of order, is stuck with the given positive order, the subject's capacity to act is hindered, since any act is suicidal; that is, it entails the collapse of order as such; the subject can act the moment he is able to resist the existing positive order *on behalf of the Order as such,* with the purpose of establishing a "better," "true" order. Or, at the level of the Oedipal complex: the subject overcomes the adolescent crisis when he resists his father in the name of the (paternal) Law itself. The space for the act is thus opened up by the gap between ordering and order.

In order to illustrate what this inversion of the standard Idealist notion of the Universal effectively amounts to, a (perhaps unexpected) reference to two recent films would be of some help. Neil Jordan's *The Crying Game* and David Cronenberg's *M Butterfly* tell the story of a man passionately in love with a woman who turns out to be another man dressed up as a woman. The moment of shock that, of course, occurs when the man finally discovers his beloved's true sexual identity can be read in two different ways. According to the first reading, *The Crying Game* and *M Butterfly* offer a tragicomic confused bundle of male fantasies about women, not a true relationship to a woman: these two films simultaneously mask and point toward the fact that what we are dealing with is a case of homosexual love for the transvestite – they are simply dishonest and refuse to acknowledge this obvious fact. Along these lines, one could propose a reading of *The Crying Game* according to which the key to the film is the hero's (Fergus's) intense, but repressed homosexual attraction to Jody, the black English soldier imprisoned by the IRA; the "implausible" resolution of this tension (Fergus doesn't kill Jody, he dies by way of accidentally colliding with an oncoming English military vehicle) has a dreamlike quality of a compromise-formation whereby the subject's wish (to get rid of the traumatic object of desire) is realized through an accident, that is, without the subject's being responsible for it.[60] After getting rid of the true, but unacceptable, object of his desire, Fergus follows the classic neurotic scenario and transfers his affection to an (apparently) acceptable person close to this object (wife, sister, or, in this case, girlfriend, the beautiful black Dil). So, when Fergus discovers that Dil is actually a man, he as it were gets from the other the truth of his (homosexual) desire: the substitute object reveals itself too close to the true object.[61] There is, however, another, far more disturbing reading: what if this displacement from the true (homosexual) object to an idealized Lady is not merely a case of false heterosexual love that disguises a true homosexual attachment, but the truth, the underlying libidinal economy, of a "straight" heterosexual attachment? From this perspective, the true enigma of *The Crying Game* is: how can a hopeless love between the hero and his partner, a man dressed up as a woman, realize the notion of heterosexual love far more "authentically" than a "normal" relationship to a woman? In this way, the ending of *The Crying Game* could be read as adding an unexpected turn of the screw to the famous punchline that ends *Some Like It Hot,* the love-sick millionaire answering the last, desperate argument of Daphne (Jack Lemmon) against their marriage ("But I'm a man, not a woman!") with the stoic and forgiving "Well, nobody's perfect!"[62] In *The Crying Game,* the fact that the partner is a man effectively doesn't disturb the relationship. That is to say, the first reading remains within the abstract opposition of the heterosexual norm and homosexuality qua its "transgressive" inversion, whereas the second reading reveals the secret of the norm itself: it renders visible the uncanny fact that, in the male fantasy that supports the "normal" heterosexual relationship, man's partner, *the* Woman about whom he is dreaming, is another man dressed up as a woman, and what – unconsciously, at least – turns him on is the very awareness of this fact. In other words, in the "heterosexual" male fantasmatic space, there are only male subjects: sexual difference amounts to a mere masquerade. It is only here that we accomplish the "inversion of inversion": when we acknowledge the "perverted" fantasmatic support of the (heterosexual) norm itself.

This paradoxical fantasmatic status of "straight" sex is grounded in Lacan's displacement of the standard classification of sexuality, of its division into "straight" heterosexuality and homosexuality that is then further subdivided into gay and lesbian sexuality. Lacan divides sexuality into the only true *hetero*sexuality, that is, lesbian sex, the only one in which the otherness of our partner is maintained, in which we truly relate to the Other Sex, and homosexuality, which is then further subdivided into gay sexuality and "straight" heterosexuality. In both cases, the partner is reduced to the "same," since, as we have just seen, the hidden fantasm that supports straight sex is that our feminine partner is a man dressed up as a woman. Or, to put it even more pointedly: the only "pure" sexual difference is the difference between (gay) homosexuality and (lesbian) heterosexuality, whereas "straight" heterosexuality, far from being the "norm," functions as an uncanny surplus, as a disturbing stain, the outcome of the confusion of a faked otherness in which the same-sexed partner, a man, is masked as a woman. In short, it is "straight" sex that is the original "deviation."

If, then, a woman is perceived by her partner in the "straight" sexual relation as a man masked as woman, does this not prove that the notion of femininity as masquerade is fundamentally a male fantasy according to which there is only one sex, male – if we scratch the surface of the mask, we discover a man beneath a woman, like the animal (cat, fox, bear) in cartoons or fairy tales who can take off its fur and disclose its human skin (see also the proverbial ideological statement that, beneath their yellow skin, all Vietnamese men are really Americans)? The answer is no: what the male fantasy of a woman as masked man conceals is not the true feminine substance but the fact that there is *nothing* beneath the (feminine) mask – the fantasy of a male subject beneath the feminine mask is a desperate endeavor to avoid the "nothingness" beneath the mask that "is" the subject.

FROM SCHELLING TO VIRTUAL REALITY
Through this unavoidable role of semblance in the subject's relating to reality, we have reached the other aspect of the problem of

"phenomenalization," this crux of Schelling's philosophical endeavor: not only the emergence of the Word, but also the emergence of the fantasmatic space of pure semblance that cannot be reduced to bodily reality. Let's resort to another literary example. In J. G. Ballard's short story "The Gioconda of the Twilight Noon," the hero, recovering from an eye disease, spends his days in a deck chair close to the seashore, listening to the sounds of the gulls, immobilized due to the bandage covering his eyes. The sounds of the gulls repeatedly evoke in him a strange magic scene in the course of which he climbs the stairs of a mysterious sea-cave, at the top of which a half-veiled woman, the ultimate incestuous object of desire, is awaiting him (the last line of the story characterizes the hero as "an eager, unrepentant Oedipus"); however, he always awakens just before the woman's identity is revealed. When, finally, the doctor proclaims him cured and takes off his bandage, the scene no longer appears to him; in despair, he makes a radical choice, steps outside at noon and looks straight at the sun until he goes blind, hoping that, in this way, he will be able to view the scene in its entirety. This story stages the choice between reality and the fantasmatic real accessible only to a blinded subject. The gap between the two is that of anamorphosis: from the standpoint of reality, the real is nothing but a formless stain, whereas the view of the fantasmatic real blurs the contours of "reality."

The *dispositif* of Ballard's story is none other than that of Plato's myth of the cave from his *Republic* (which, incidentally, is also a cinematographic dispositif *avant la lettre*). How are we to modify this basic idealist dispositif in order to get a *materialist* dispositif? According to materialism, the status of true reality (of the sun outside the cave) beyond the bodily reality of the cave is that of an anamorphic fantasy, of something that can never be perceived directly, but only through its distorted reflection on the empty wall of the cave that serves as its "screen." The true line of separation thus runs within the cave itself, between the material reality the cavemen see around themselves, and the elusive "anamorphic" appearance of the "suprasensible," "incorporeal" event on the wall of the cave – as was emphasized by Lacan (and, well before him, by Hegel), the suprasensible is appearance as appear-

57

ance. Or, to put it in yet another way: if the main problem of idealism is how we are to pass from the ever-changing "false" material phenomenal reality to the true reality of Ideas (from the cave in which we can perceive only shadows to the daylight in which we can catch a glimpse of sun), the problem of materialism from Lucretius through Schelling's *Weltalter* and the Marxist notion of commodity fetishism to Deleuze's "logic of sense" is the exact opposite, namely *the genesis of the semblance itself*: how does the reality of bodies generate out of itself the fantasmatic surface, the "incorporeal" sense event?

The minimal dispositif of the relationship between signifier, reality, and the fantasmatic Real is provided by Saki's famous short story "Window": a guest arrives at a country house and looks through the spacious French window at the field behind the house; the daughter of the family, alone at home and thus the only one to receive him, tells him that she now lives alone in the house – all other members of the family died recently in an accident. Soon afterward, when the guest looks through the window again, he sees the members of the family approaching slowly across the field, returning from the hunt; convinced that what he sees are ghosts of the deceased, he runs away in horror. (The daughter, of course, is a clever pathological liar; for her family, she quickly concocts another story to explain why the guest left the house in a panic.) So, a few words providing the proper symbolic context suffice to transform the window into a fantasy frame and to transubstantiate miraculously the muddy tenants into frightful apparitions. At a more elaborate level, one finds the same dispositif in one of the better recent science fiction films, Roland Emmerich's *Stargate,* the story of a young scientist who solves the enigma of a gigantic ring made of unknown metal, discovered in Egypt in the 1920s: after one enters the appropriate seven symbols, the ring starts to function as a "stargate" – by stepping through the hole in its middle, one enters another, alternative universe, that is, a different time-space dimension. What makes the ring operative is the identification of the missing seventh symbol: we are thus dealing with symbolic efficiency, not with a scientific inquiry into material causality. It is the inscription of the appropriate symbols that activates the ring in its capacity of the fantasmatic frame, as in Saki's "Window," where the symbolic intervention transubstantiates the ordinary window frame into a screen of fantasmatic apparitions.[63] What is crucial here is the topological structure of this dispositif: not only the hole in reality that functions as the opening to the Other Scene of fantasy, but also a kind of topological twist, turning-into-itself, of reality, best exemplified by the theatrical stage: if we look at it from a spectator's seat, we are engrossed in the fantasmatic space, whereas if we go backstage, we are immediately struck by the poverty of the mechanism responsible for the stage illusion – the fantasmatic space dissipates, "there is nothing to see" . . .

In science fiction literature and cinema, a mirror, a window or a door often serves as the passage into the other, fantasmatic dimension: one of the standard scenes in science fiction is that of a subject who opens up a door and, instead of the expected reality beyond its threshold, encounters something wholly unexpected (a ghastly real) – the secret is often "the secret beyond the door." In another version of the same procedure, the subject looks into the mirror and sees in it "something else," not the reflection of everyday reality this side of the mirror. (In one of the stories of the English omnibus *Dead of the Night* from 1945, the hero casts a glance into the mirror in his common modern bedroom – what he sees there is another dark, "Gothic" room with antiquated furniture and a burning fireplace.) In the history of cinema, perhaps the greatest master of this art of elevating an everyday door or window into the fantasmatic place of passage was Orson Welles; in his version of Kafka's *The Trial*, for example, he systematically exploits the fantasmating potential of the simple act of opening a door: "Always they open onto bewilderingly different places. . . . The 'next room' in *The Trial* always suggests a repressed psychic horror."[64] When the ordinary woman doing her laundry in a decayed room opens up the small doors at the bottom of the room and ushers K. through it, K. all of a sudden finds himself in a large room in which something like a political rally is going on, with hundreds of people packed in the rafters and the air thick with smoke. The adventure that befalls K. in his office building stands in a clear contrast to this sudden passage from a small private space into a large public space: walking along a brilliantly lit cor-

ridor in the large and modern office building, K. opens the door
to a tiny storage closet, where he finds a man in leather whipping
two corrupt policemen against whom he earlier laid a complaint:
"The huge corporate workroom has given way to a claustrophobic
torture chamber, an ugly little space lit with a naked bulb and
filled with cringing figures."[65] This scene renders perfectly the
twisted logic of the superego: it culpabilizes K. by merely realizing, in an excessively literal way, his own complaint against the
policemen – in the guise of the obscene, sadomasochistic sex-
ualized torture, K. receives the truth of his own demand to the
Other of the Law.

And is not this *dispositif* – the frame through which one can
glimpse the Other Scene – the elementary *dispositif* of fantasmatic space from prehistoric Lascaux paintings to computer-
generated Virtual Reality? Is not the *interface* of a computer the
last materialization of this frame? What defines the properly "human dimension" is the presence of a screen, a frame, through
which we communicate with the "suprasensible" virtual universe
to be found nowhere in reality: it was already Lacan who pointed
out that the proper place of Plato's Ideas is the surface of pure
appearance. This hole derails the balance of our embeddedness in
the natural environs and throws us into the state of being "out of
joint" described by Schelling: no longer "at home" in the material
world, striving for the Other Scene that, however, remains forever "virtual," a promise of itself, a fleeting anamorphic glimmer
accessible only to a side view. The point is not only that man is a
zoon techniko, interposing artificial technological environs, his
"second nature," between himself and his raw natural environs; it
is rather that the status of this "second nature" is irreducibly *virtual.* To go back to the example of interface: "virtual" is the space
we see on the screen of the interface, this universe of signs and
splendid images through which we can freely surf, the universe
projected onto the screen and creating on it a false impression of
"depth." The moment we cross its threshold and take a look at
what lies "effectively" behind the screen, we encounter nothing
but senseless digital machinery. This fantasmatic scene and the
symbolic order are strictly correlative: there is no symbolic order
without the fantasmatic space, no ideal order of *logos* without the

pseudomaterial, "virtual," Other Scene where the fantasmatic apparitions can emerge, or, as Schelling put it, there is no Spirit without Spirits, no pure spiritual universe of Ideas without the obscene, ethereal, fantasmatic corporeality of "spirits" (undead, ghosts, vampires . . .). Therein, in this assertion of the unavoidable pseudomaterial fantasmatic support of Ideas, resides the crucial insight of true ("dialectical") materialism.

What is a fantasy screen, an "interface?" Sometimes we find it even in nature, as in the case of Cerknica Lake in Slovenia: this intermittent lake (during its seasonal eruption, water throws into the air fishes, etc.) was experienced as a kind of magic screen, a miracle of something emerging out of a void. As early as the seventeenth century, this phenomenon intrigued natural scientists. A Slovene author, Janez Valvasor, became a member of the English Royal Academy for providing an explanation of this mystery (an intricate network of underground channels with different pressures). Perhaps this is the most elementary definition of a *mechanism:* a machine that produces an *effect* in the precise sense of "magical" effect of sense, of an event that involves a gap between itself and the raw bodily materiality – mechanism is that which accounts for the emergence of an "illusion." The crucial point here is that the insight into the mechanism does *not* destroy the illusion, the "effect"; it even strengthens it insofar as it renders palpable the gap between the bodily causes and their surface effect (suffice it to recall the recent series of "The making of . . . " films that accompany the big-budget productions – *Terminator 2, Indiana Jones,* etc.). The same goes more and more for political-campaign ads and publicity in general: first the stress was on the product (or candidate) itself, then it moved to the effect-image, while now it is shifting more and more to the making of the image (the strategy of making an ad is itself advertized, etc.). The paradox is that – in a kind of reversal of the old cliché according to which Western ideology dissimulates the production process at the expense of the final product – the production process, far from being the secret locus of the prohibited, of what cannot be shown, of what is concealed by the fetish, serves as the fetish that fascinates with its presence.[66]

It was Gilles Deleuze – another great Schellingian – who, long

before the fashion of Virtual Reality, elaborated the status of virtuality apropos of the mystery of *event*. From the prehistoric
paintings on the walls of the Lascaux caves to virtual reality, we
confront the same enigma: how is it possible for us to suspend
reality and become engrossed in the virtual space of the fantasmatic screen? How can the "incorporeal" event emerge out of the
mixture of bodies, of bodily causes?[67] We seem to know everything about the social and artistic background of film noir: the
traumatic impact of World War II on the established gender roles,
the influence of German expressionism, etc., etc. – but all this is
clearly not sufficient to account for the emergence of the noir
universe with its unique flavor of all-permeating corruption embodied in the figure of the femme fatale. It is the same with
courtly love: one can play indefinitely the historicist game of
sources and influences: the hidden reference to Arab esoteric tra-
ditions; the incestuous triangle of the knight, his Lady, and the
paternal figure of her husband; the difficult situation of the
disposessed knight in disintegrating feudalism; etc., etc. There is,
however, an insurmountable gap, a "nothing," that separates forever this mixture of material causes from the event of the mirac-
ulous emergence of the Lady. This Deleuzian claim that the sense
event cannot be reduced to the mixture of bodily causes also allows us to locate properly the Foucauldian project of "archaeology": what Foucault aims at is not the reduction of an event to the
network of its causes (no matter how heterogeneous and contingent they are), but the rules of the emergence and disap-
pearance of events, rules whose status is totally different from the
laws that regulate the mixture of bodily causes and effects.

The key for the status of Virtual Reality is provided by the
difference between imitation and simulation:[68] Virtual Reality
doesn't *imitate* reality, it *simulates* it by way of generating its semblance. In other words, imitation imitates a preexisting real-life
model, whereas simulation generates the semblance of a nonex-
isting reality – it simulates something that doesn't exist. Let us
take the most elementary case of virtuality in a computer, so-
called virtual memory: a computer can simulate far greater memory than it actually has; that is, it can function *as if* its memory is

larger than it is. And does the same not hold for every symbolic arrangement, up to the financial system that simulates a far larger extent of coverage than it is effectively able to provide? The entire system of deposits and the like works on the presupposition that anyone can, at any moment, withdraw his or her money from the bank – a presupposition that, although it can never be realized, nonetheless renders possible the very "real," "material" functioning of the financial system.

The consequences of this difference between imitation and simulation are more radical than may appear. In contrast to imitation, which sustains belief in preexisting "organic" reality, simulation retroactively "denaturalizes" reality itself by way of disclosing the mechanism responsible for its generation.[69] In other words, the "ontological wager" of simulation is that there is no ultimate difference between nature and its artificial reproduction. There is a more elementary level of the Real with reference to which both simulated screen-reality and "real" reality are generated effects, the Real of pure computation: behind the event viewed through interface (the simulated effect of reality) there is pure subjectless ("acephalous") computation, a series of 1 and 0, of + and −. In *Seminar II*,[70] where Lacan develops for the first time this notion of the series of + and −, he reduces it precipitously to the order of the signifier; for that reason, one should reread these passages from the perspective of the opposition between signifier and letter (or writing) established in *Seminar XX*:[71] subjectless digital computation is neither the differential symbolic order (the symbolic realm of meaning is part of the pseudoreality manipulated on the screen) nor reality outside the screen of the interface (in bodily reality behind the screen, there are only chips, electric current, etc.). The wager of Virtual Reality is that the universe of meaning, of narrativization, is not the ultimate reference, the unsurpassable horizon, since it relies on pure computation. Therein resides the gap that separates forever Lacan from postmodernist deconstructionism: the latter conceives science as one of the possible local narrativizations, whereas for Lacan, contemporary science enables us to gain access to the Real of pure computation that underlies the play of multiple narrativizations. This is the Lacanian Real: the purely virtual, "not really existing," order of

63

subjectless computation that nonetheless regulates every "reality," material and/or imaginary. One can see, now, in what precise sense the status of Virtuality is ambiguous: this term refers simultaneously and in an irreducible way to the virtual status of the fantasmatic "reality" we perceive on the screen of the interface *and* to the pure computation that cannot be reduced to its materialization in the electric current running through computer chips.

Prior to Schelling, the philosopher who provided the best conceptual apparatus to account for Virtual Reality was Malebranche, with his "occasionalism." Malebranche, a disciple of Descartes, drops Descartes's ridiculous reference to the pineal gland in order to explain the coordination between the material and the spiritual substance, that is, body and soul; how, then, are we to explain their coordination, if there is no contact between the two, no point at which a soul can act causally on a body or vice versa? Since the two causal networks (that of ideas in my mind and that of bodily interconections) are totally independent, the only solution is that a third, true Substance (God) continuously coordinates and mediates between the two, sustaining the semblance of continuity: when I think about raising my hand and my hand rises, my thought causes the raising of my hand not directly but only "occasionally" – upon noticing my thought directed at raising my hand, God sets in motion the other, material, causal chain that leads to my hand effectively being raised. If we replace "God" with the big Other, the symbolic order, we can see the closeness of occasionalism to Lacan's position: as Lacan put it in his polemics against Aristotle in "Television,"[72] the relationship between soul and body is never direct, since the big Other always interposes itself between the two. Occasionalism is thus essentially a name for the "arbitrariness of the signifier," for the gap that separates the network of ideas from the network of bodily (real) causality, for the fact that it is the big Other that accounts for the coordination of the two networks, so that, when my body bites an apple, my soul experiences a pleasurable sensation. This same gap is targeted by the ancient Aztec priest who organizes human sacrifices to ensure that the sun will rise again: the human sacrifice is here an appeal to God to sustain the coordination between the two series, the bodily necessity and the concatenation of symbolic events. "Irrational" as the Aztec priest's sacrificing may appear, its underlying premise is far more insightful than our commonplace intuition according to which the coordination between body and soul is direct, that is, it is "natural" for me to have a pleasurable sensation when I bite an apple since this sensation is caused directly by the apple. What gets lost is the intermediary role of the big Other in guaranteeing the coordination between reality and our mental experience of it. And is it not the same with our immersion into Virtual Reality? When I raise my hand in order to push an object in the virtual space, this object effectively moves – my illusion, of course, is that it was the movement of my hand that directly caused the dislocation of the object; that is, in my immersion, I overlook the intricate mechanism of computerized coordination, homologous to the role of God guaranteeing the coordination between the two series in occasionalism.[73]

For that reason, it is crucial to maintain open the radical ambiguity of how cyberspace will affect our lives: this does not depend on technology as such but on the mode of its social inscription. Immersion into cyberspace can intensify our bodily experience (new sensuality, new body with more organs, new sexes . . .), but it also opens up the possibility for the one who manipulates the machinery that runs the cyberspace literally to *steal* our own (virtual) body, depriving us of the control over it, so that one no longer relates to one's body as to "one's own." What one encounters here is the constitutive ambiguity of the notion of mediatization:[74] originally this notion designated the gesture by means of which a subject was stripped of its direct, immediate right to make decisions; the great master of political mediatization was Napoleon, who left to the conquered monarchs the appearance of power, while they were effectively no longer in a position to exercise it. At a more general level, one could say that such a "mediatization" of the monarch defines constitutional monarchy: in it, the monarch is reduced to the point of a purely formal symbolic gesture of "dotting the i's," of signing and thus conferring the performative force on the edicts whose content is determined by the elected governing body. And does the same *mutatis mutandis* also not hold for today's progressive computerization of our everyday lives, in the course of which the subject is also more and more "mediatized," imperceptibly stripped of power, under the false guise of its increase? When our body is mediatized (caught in the network of electronic media), it is simultaneously exposed to the threat of a radical "proletarianization": the subject is potentially reduced to the pure $, since even my own personal experience can be stolen, manipulated, regulated by the machinelike Other. One can see, again, how the prospect of radical virtualization bestows on the computer the position that is strictly homologous to that of God in Malebrancheian occasionalism: since the computer coordinates the relationship between my mind and (what I experience as) the movement of my limbs (in virtual reality), one can easily imagine a computer that runs amok and starts to act like an Evil God, disturbing the coordination between my mind and my bodily self-experience – when the signal of my mind to raise my hand is suspended or even counteracted in (virtual) reality, the most fundamental experience of the body as "mine" is undermined. It thus seems that cyberspace effectively realizes the paranoiac fantasy elaborated by Schreber, the German judge whose memoirs were analyzed by Freud:[75] the "wired universe" is psychotic insofar as it seems to materialize Schreber's hallucination of the divine rays through which God directly controls the human mind. In other words, does the externalization of the big Other in the computer not account for the inherent paranoiac dimension of the wired universe? Or, to put it in a yet another way: the commonplace is that, in cyberspace, the ability to download consciousness into a computer finally frees people from their bodies – *but it also frees the machines from "their" people* . . .

With reference to the mirror relationship between the dispersed "me" and my mirror image, this means that, in the wired universe of Virtual Reality, my mirror image is externalized in the machine, in the guise of a stand-in that replaces me in cyberspace, so that the body that is "mine" in "real life" is more and more reduced to an excremental remainder. The crucial point is thus to persist in the utter ambiguity: yes, there is an "indivisible remainder," we can never cut the links from our real

66

body and float freely in the cyberspace; since, however, our bodily self-experience itself is always-already "virtual," symbolically mediated, this body to which we are forced to return is not the constituted body of the full self-experience, of "true reality," but the formless remainder, the horror of the Real.

WHAT IS A MASTER?

The conclusion to be drawn is that, notwithstanding all the talk about "the end of the Cartesian paradigm," we continue to dwell within these conceptual coordinates. According to Fredric Jameson,[76] one of the antinomies of postmodernity is the antinomy of constructionism and essentialism: on the one hand, the vertiginous progression of universal "virtualization," the notion, more and more impending, that everything is (socially, symbolically, technically . . .) "constructed," contingent, lacking any guarantee in a preexisting ground; on the other hand, the desperate search for a firm foundation whose foremost expressions are not different religious or ethnic "fundamentalisms" but rather the return to Nature in the contemporary ecological stance. Within the domain of the postmodern New Age anti-Cartesianism, this antinomy assumes the shape of the tension between so-called Deep Ecology and New Age technospiritualism: the first advocates a return to the spontaneous experience of nature by way of breaking with the attitude of technological domination, whereas the second sets its hopes on a spiritual reversal brought about by the very opposite, the complete technological reproduction of reality (the notion that, in some not too distant future, by way of their full immersion into Virtual Reality, human subjects will be able to weigh the anchor that attaches them to their bodies and to change into ghostlike entities floating freely from one virtual body to another).

It is thus easy to discern the crux of the attraction exerted by the ecological stance: it presents itself as the only credible answer to the *hubris* of the modern subject, to the permanent instability built into capitalist logic. That is to say, *the* problem of today's ethics is how to install a Limit in our universe of postmodern relativism in which no agency possesses the unconditional authority to tell us you can go "So far and no further." Ecology emerges here as the only serious contender against postmodern relativism: it offers *nature itself,* the fragile balance of the Earth's ecosystem, as the point of reference providing the proper Measure, the unsurpassable Limit, for our acts – *this gesture of procuring an "objective" justification for the Limit is ideology at its purest.* Against the deep-ecological reassertion of the Limit, one should therefore vindicate Schelling's seemingly "pessimist," "reactionary," insight that the universe as such is "out of joint," that a radical dislocation is its positive ontological condition.[77] Or, with reference to the Schellingian antagonism of contraction and expansion: is Virtual Reality not the extreme form of *expansion,* of the loss of our anchorage in the contracted physical body? And is ecology not a no less extreme *contractive* reaction to this loss? We can return now to the opposition between Deep Ecology and New Age technospiritualism: the fantasy of the reestablished natural balance with humanity relegated to its subordinated part and the fantasy of the evaporation of bodily inertia in comprehensive virtualization are two opposed strategies to disavow the *splitting* between what we call "reality" and the void of the Real filled by a fantasmatic content, that is, the elusive, intangible gap that sustains "reality."

Insofar as the impact of Virtual Reality is rooted in the dynamics of capitalism, it is no wonder that Marx's analysis of capitalism, his emphasis on the necessary codependence between lack and excess, remains pertinent for our approach to Virtual Reality. As was pointed out already by Hegel in his theory of civil society, the paradox of modern poverty is that the lack of wealth does not depend on society's limited productive capacities, but is generated by the very excess of production, by "too much wealth" – surplus and lack are correlative. Lack (the poverty of the "rabble") is the very form of appearance of the excess of production. On that account, any attempt to "balance" the lack and the excess (and what is Fascism, in its economic policy, if not a desperate attempt to reintroduce a fundamental balance into the cycle of social [re]production) is doomed to fail: the very attempt to abolish lack (poverty) by producing more wealth leads to more poverty . . . On a somewhat different level, we encounter a homologous codependence of lack and excess in the Stalinist version of "totalitarianism": how does the superego function in the Stalinist bureaucratic universe? The supreme examples of it, of course, are the Stalinist purges. The double bind that pertains to the very notion of superego is best embodied in the fate of Stalin's ministers of the interior – Yezhov, Yagoda, Abakoumov. There was a constant pressure on them to discover ever new anti-Socialist plots, they were always reproached for being too lenient, not vigilant enough; the only way for them to satisfy the demand of the Leader was thus to invent plots and to arrest innocent people. However, this way, they were laying the ground for their own violent demise, since their successor was already at work, collecting evidence of how they were actually counterrevolutionary agents of imperialism killing good dedicated bolsheviks . . . The victim's innocence is thus part of the game, it enables the self-reproducing cycle of revolutionary purges that "eat their own children." This impossibility of achieving the "proper measure" between lack and excess (of zeal in the fight against counterrevolution) is the clearest index of the superego functioning of the Stalinist bureaucracy: we are either too lenient (if we do not discover enough traitors, this proves our silent support for counterrevolution) or too vigilant (which, again, makes us guilty of condemning dedicated fighters for Socialism).[78] This codependence of lack and excess is, perhaps, the core of what we call "modernity."[79]

Another case of the codependence between lack and excess is provided by the paradoxical role of the "narrow band" (the fact that, for structural reasons, the picture is always limited, reduced) in the process of symbolization: it is this lack, this *limitation* itself, that activates the *excessive* wealth of imagination (suffice it to recall the almost proverbial example of a child with simple wooden toys, whose imagination is far superior to the one playing with intricate electronic equipment). Therein resides the impasse of the complete immersion into Virtual Reality: it saturates the force of imagination, since everything is already rendered to our eyes. This also accounts for the structural impasse of so-called interactive storytelling in which, at every turn of the story, the reader is free to select his or her own version of the events (the hero can win over or lose the desired lady, etc.). Experience shows that such a constellation gives rise to a double discontent in the reader: (1) there is "too much freedom," too much depends on me; instead of yielding to the pleasures of the narrative, I am bombarded with decisions to be made; (2) my naive faith in diegetic reality is disturbed, that is, to the horror of the official ideology of interactive storytelling, I read a story in order to learn what "really" happened to the hero (did he "really" win over the coveted lady, etc.), not in order to decide about the outcome.[80] What underlies this frustration is the demand for a *Master*: in a narrative, I *want* somebody to establish the rules and assume responsibility for the course of the events – excessive freedom is frustrating to the utmost. More than an answer to the threat of an actual ecological catastrophe, Deep Ecology is an attempt to counter this lack of an "objective," imposed set of rules that limits our freedom. What one should bear in mind here is the link between this limitation and our "sense of reality": in the interactive virtual universe, reality lacks its inherent limitation and is thus, as it were, deprived of its substance, changed into a kind of ethereal image of itself.

What implicit rule is then actually violated in an "interactive" narrative? When we watch a performance of *Othello,* we know well what lies ahead, yet we are nonetheless full of anxiety and again and again shocked at the tragic outcome, as if, at another level, we were not quite sure that the inevitable would happen again. Do we not encounter here a new variation on the motif of the prohibition of the impossible and/or of the injunction to do what is already in itself necessary? Of the gap that separates the two deaths, symbolic and real? The gap exemplified by the ancient Aztec priest who organizes human sacrifices to ensure the rising of the sun, who is alarmed by the seemingly "irrational" prospect that the most obvious thing will not happen? And is not the same gesture of freely asserting the inevitable constitutive of the position of a Master? By means of his "Yes!" a Master merely "dots the i's," attests the unavoidable – he acts as if he has a choice where effectively there is none. (For that reason, there is unavoidably something inherently *asinine* involved in the position of a Master: a Master's main role is to *state the obvious.*) Suffice it to recall today's relationship between the Western great powers and Russia: in accordance with the silent pact regulating this relationship, Western states treat Russia as a great power on condition that Russia doesn't (effectively) act as one. One can see how the logic of the offer made to be rejected (Russia is offered the chance to act as a great power, on condition that it politely rejects this offer) is connected with a possibility that has to remain a mere possibility: in principle, it is possible for Russia to act effectively as a great power, but if Russia is to maintain the symbolic status of a great power, this possiblity must not be taken advantage of . . . Is, therefore, Russia's position not the position of Master as such? Another aspect of this same paradoxical position of Master concerns the enigma of passing exams and the announcement of their results: there has to be a minimal gap, delay, between the actual examination, the direct measurement of our capacities, and the moment of public proclamation of the result – an in between time when, although the die is already cast and we know it, there is nonetheless an "irrational" uncertainty as to "what will the Master (proclaiming the results) say," as if it is only via its public proclamation that the result becomes actual, "for itself."[81]

The tautological emptiness of a Master's Wisdom is exemplified in the inherent stupidity of proverbs. Let us engage in a mental experiment by way of trying to construct proverbial wisdom out of the relationship between terrestrial life, its pleasures, and its Beyond. If one says "Forget about the afterlife, about the Elsewhere, seize the day, enjoy life fully here and now, it's the only life you've got!" it sounds deep. If one says exactly the opposite ("Do not get trapped in the illusory and vain pleasures of earthly life; money, power, and passions are all destined to vanish into thin air – think about eternity!"), it also sounds deep. If one combines the two sides ("Bring Eternity into your everyday life, live your life on this earth as if it is already permeated by Eternity!"), we get another profound thought. Needless to add, the same goes for its inversion: "Do not try in vain to bring together Eternity and your terrestrial life, accept humbly that you are forever split between Heaven and Earth!" If, finally, one simply gets perplexed by all these reversals and claims: "Life is an enigma, do not try to penetrate its secrets, accept the beauty of its unfathomable mystery!" the result is, again, no less profound than its reversal: "Do not allow yourself to be distracted by false mysteries that just dissimulate the fact that, ultimately, life is very simple – it is what it is, it is simply here without reason and rhyme!" Needless to add that, by uniting mystery and simplicity, one again obtains a wisdom: "The ultimate, unfathomable mystery of life resides in its very simplicity, in the simple fact that there is life."

This tautological imbecility points toward the fact that a Master is excluded from the economy of symbolic exchange – not wholly excluded, since he occupies a special, exceptional place in it. For the Master, there is no "tit for tat," since, for him, tit is in a way *already its own tat*. In other words, when we give something to the Master, we do not expect anything in return, since this gift to the Master functions as its own reward – we are honored when the Master accepts our gift. Is it not often the case, with the persons toward whom we entertain a relationship of transference, that they do us a favor by merely accepting our gift?[82] This refusal to be caught in the circle of exchange is what ultimately defines the attitude of a Master: the decline of the figure of Master in modern capitalist societies follows inherently from the definition of modern society as the society of *exchange*. Even when Masters seem to participate in an act of exchange, they are actually consummating the paradoxical *exchange of gifts* that doesn't yet function as the proper act of exchange: in the ritual of *potlatch,* for example, when I endeavor to organize an even more sumptuous feast for my guest than he did previously for me, the point is not to "reimburse the debt" but to repeat and outdo the excess of the gift.

So what is a Master? The conductor of an orchestra, for example: what he does is in a sense superfluous, that is, a perfectly rehearsed orchestra would have no need for the conductor. Precisely as such – as superfluous – the conductor adds the crucial je ne sais quoi, the unfathomable tact and accent. *The Master thus gives body to the irreducible excess of contingency over Necessity* – when the playing of the orchestra follows with full necessity, the master-conductor is no longer needed. The gesture constitutive of the Master is best exemplified by a tense political situation in which a leader is torn between two options: either to assert a proper position in its extreme purity or to formulate a position broadly enough in order to present it as a wide "umbrella" able to embrace all currents of the leader's party. The outcome is utterly "undecidable": adopting the unreconciliable "extreme" stance can isolate the leader, it can make him or her appear unacceptable, yet it can also be perceived as the resolute measure that clearly designates the desired Goal and thus attracts broad masses (see General de Gaulle's resolute "No!" to collaboration with Germans in 1940 that made him into a leader); adopting the ill-defined "umbrella" stance can lay ground for a broad coalition, yet it can also be perceived as the disappointing sign of irresolution. Sometimes it is better to limit oneself pragmatically to "realistic," attainable goals; at other times, it is far more effective to say, "No, this is not enough, the true utopia is that, in the present state of our society, we can achieve even these modest goals – if we want truly to attain even these goals, we must aim much higher, we must change the general condition!" This, perhaps, is the feature that distinguishes a "true leader": the ability to risk the step into the extreme that, far from ostracizing the leader, *finds universal appeal and grounds the widest possible coalition.* Such a gesture, of course, is extremely risky insofar as it is not decideable in advance: it *can* succeed, yet it *can* also turn the leader into a figure of ridicule, a lone extremist nut. This is the risk a "true leader" has to assume: one of the lessons of history is that, in the political struggle between the moderate pragmatic and the extremist, it was the extremist who (later, after taking over) was able effectively to realize the necessary pragmatic measures.

There is a logical game that can further clarify the paradox of the Master:[83] two persons, A and B; both bear on their head a cardinal number visible only to the other person; one number is always a successor or a forerunner to the other number, so that, if one person bears a number 5, the other's number is necessarily either 4 or 6; 0 is forbidden. How, then, can the two persons arrive at knowledge of their respective number? Let us reproduce three basic situations:

A has 1, B has 2, that is, A sees on B 2, B sees on A 1. This combination, of course, renders possible the immediate insight of B: A sees 2 on B and cannot immediately guess what is on her head, 1 or 3, whereas B, who sees 1 on A, knows immediately that he bears 2. B is thus able to arrive at the answer directly: his knowledge is not mediated by the nonknowledge of A.

A has 2, B has 3. Here, it is again B who first arrives at the answer, but *his knowledge is mediated by A's ignorance.* That is to say, the reasoning proceeds in two steps: (1) A sees 3 and doesn't know her number (2 or 4), so she says, "I don't know"; (2) B sees 2 and says to himself, "I have either 1 or 3; if I were to have 1, A would know she has 2; since, however, A doesn't know her number, it follows that I have 3."

A has 3, B has 4. It is again B who first arrives at the answer; however, the reasoning now has to go through three steps:

(1) B sees 3 and doesn't know his number (2 or 4), so he states his ignorance;

(2) A sees 4 and doesn't know her number (3 or 5); B's ignorance is of no help to her here – since A sees 4, she knows that B sees on her either 3 or 5, and thus knows in advance that B's first answer will be "I don't know" (i.e., if B sees either 3 or 5, in both cases he cannot directly guess his number);

(3) on the basis of this *double* profession of ignorance, however, B is able, in the third step, to arrive at knowledge. His reasoning is: "I see 3 on A, so I have either 2 or 4 – I do not know my number, and A is aware of my ignorance. However, if I were to have 2, A should be able to arrive at her number on the basis of my ignorance. That is to say, if I were to have 2, A's reasoning would be: 'I see 2 on B; this means that I have either 1 or 3. If I were to have 1, B would know that he has 2. Since, however, B doesn't know his number, I have 3.' Since, however, A doesn't know her number, my number must be 4." In other words, the ignorance of B (the fact that B who sees 3 on A doesn't know if his number is 2 or 4) assumes a different meaning/value for A with regard to what she sees on B: if A sees on B 2, B's ignorance tells her that she has 3; if A sees on B 4, B's ignorance tells her that she has either 3 or 5, that is, it tells her nothing she doesn't know already prior to B's profession of ignorance. To resume the reasoning of B: "I see 3 on

A, so I have 2 or 4 – I do not know what I have. However, if
I were to have 2, my ignorance would tell A that she has 3;
since A doesn't know that she has 3, my number must be
4." B takes into account the effect of his (profession of)
ignorance on A: if B's profession of ignorance produces
knowledge in A, he has 2, if not, he has 4.

It is easy to discern in these three figurations the triad of the social
link of the Master, the University, and Analysis: in the link of the
Master, the Servant directly recognizes who is "numero uno" and
thus assumes a subservient role; in the link of the University, the
knowledge of the person of the university is mediated by the
ignorance of the Other; in the link of Analysis, the analysand
arrives at the knowledge (about the truth of the analysand's
desire) through an initial profession of ignorance and the following profession of ignorance of the analyst – the analyst must not
directly act as the one who knows, but rather as the one who
stands for the lack in the Other, for the big Other's ignorance. In
this precise sense, the analyst has to be able to count to 4, as
Lacan put it. However, even more interesting than this is an enigmatic feature of the third figuration: the first step in the process of
reasoning is B's proclamation of his ignorance; the enigma of this
step is that it is necessary, that is, unavoidable, but, at the same
time, *totally superfluous* – B states something that A already
knows; that is, since A sees 4 on B, she knows in advance that the
first gesture of B can only be his profession of ignorance. However, if B doesn't begin by stating the obvious, if the game begins
directly with A's stating "I don't know," B cannot arrive at his
knowledge. Here one encounters the symbolic order at its purest:
the purely superfluous gesture of stating the obvious. This necessity to begin by stating the obvious is a kind of ontological proof
of the big Other; that is to say, if each of the two persons par-
ticipating knows it, who has to be informed about it? The big
Other, of course . . .

This initial gesture that, precisely insofar as it is superfluous
and "stupid," grounds the ensuing Order, is the gesture of the
Master at its purest: the "Master" is the subject who makes this
kind of "obvious" statement. In other words, the ultimate support
of the Master resides in a kernel of ignorance: in contrast to the

Enlightenment motto Knowledge is Power, *savoir est pouvoir,* one should assert that, in a social link, the position of the Master always relies on a minimum of ignorance, of *je n'en veux rien savoir.* From the proverbial Potemkin's villages to the model socialist villages hastily constructed along the main rail line in China to conceal the failure of the Great Leap Forward in 1959 from Mao Tse-tung's gaze, what we encounter again and again is the urge to conceal from the Master's gaze the grayness of everyday life. And the crucial point is that this ignorance is constitutive: the Master's decision is never fully "grounded in reasons"; there is always a minimum of arbitrariness and sheer idiocy in it. Therein resides the tragedy of Enlightened leftists who are unable to take into account this constitutive role of idiotic symbolic rituals (from Reagan to Tudjman in Croatia) and indulge in mocking them.

RECONCILIATION

The gap between the Real of the act and its symbolic assumption by means of which the act only becomes "itself" – in Hegelian terms, the gap between the "In-itself" and the "For-itself," the delay of the symbolic gesture of "freely choosing" with regard to the deed, on account of which the choice is ultimately always a forced one, an act of assuming what is already imposed on us – has profound consequences for Schelling's notion of divine freedom: as was pointed out by Marquet, the fact that God pronounces the Word and thus establishes himself as a free subject after being caught in the vortex of the rotary motion of blind drives means that God himself is not exempted from the predicament of the forced choice – he also is forced to assume freely what has already occurred by blind necessity. Paraphrasing Marx's famous beginning of the *Eighteenth brumaire,* one is tempted to say that, in his free act of Creation, "God makes his own history; but he does not make it just as he pleases; he does not make it under circumstances chosen by himself, but under circumstances directly encountered, given and transmitted from the past" – from the eternal Past of the rotary motion of divine prehistory. Insofar as this predicament is the necessary outcome of the ontological edifice of *Weltalter,* one can claim that the ultimate reason for the failure of the *Weltalter* project, for Schelling's retreat into the safe waters of the Aristotelian ontological frame, resides in his unreadiness to accept the fact that God's freedom is also the freedom of a forced choice, the gesture of freely assuming an imposed necessity.

In what, then, would Schelling's third "divine age," the final reconciliation between Past and Present in the reign of Love, consist? The already-mentioned "posthumanist" utopia of a new "bionic angel," of a wired subject who, by means of "downloading" consciousness into the machine, cuts the links that attach the subject to the material body and turns into a spirit freely floating in the ethereal materiality of cyberspace,[84] seems to fit perfectly the Schellingian Idealist fantasy of the third "divine age" as the redemption from the Fall, as the step from the Fall into Bliss: the fantasy of the humanity that overcomes the egotism of the contraction-into-self and thus gets rid of the material inertia, changing the bodily reality into a transparent medium of spiritual communion.

It is easy to assert here that, at some point, the subject is compelled to leave the staged illusion of cyberspace and return back to the "true reality" – say, what if the machine, the hardware support of the cyberspace, simply breaks down and throws us back to the misery of our bodily existence? However, what *is* this "true reality" of our bodily existence? Is not the fundamental lesson of Lacan that this "true reality" itself is supported by the virtual order of the big Other? In short, there is something wrong with the reasoning that tells us that we always remain attached to our body in material reality: we have to approach the problem from the opposite direction. The point to be made is not that it is not possible to cut the umbilical cord that links us to bodily reality and to float freely in virtual space, but its exact opposite: how is it that we are never fully immersed in this bodily reality, how is it that *there is no "reality" without the empty screen onto which we project fantasies?* "Reality" itself, to which we are compelled to return after every virtual escapade, needs the fantasmatic frame as the ultimate support of its consistency. The two propositions are thus to be thought together: there is no "hard reality" to which one can simply return, but there is nonetheless some "real" that prevents us from freely floating from one to another virtual body in the fantasy space. There is no reality without the blank, the screen onto which we project fantasies, since – if reality is to emerge – something must be excluded from it: the blank screen is the index of that exclusion ("primordial repression"). *The fascinating presence of a fantasy formation does not dissimulate reality: it dissimulates the void of that which had to be foreclosed if reality was to emerge.*

Is, however, this reading of the Schellingian Third Age – the Future, the return to the Divine Bliss – as simply another version of the fantasmatic dissimulation of the real, the only one possible? Schelling is well aware that, if reality is to emerge, something (the horror of the primordial vortex of drives) has to be "repressed" into the Past. The crucial point is that Schelling here parts from the mainstream of German Idealism, inclusive of his own early philosophy of identity, which conceives Law (the objective rationality of the social order experienced by the isolated egotist individual as an alien force encroaching upon his or her freedom) as the inherent condition of Love (of authentic interpersonal relations): the pressure of Law compels us to renounce narcissistic self-will and thus to discover the true love of others. Far from functioning as an impediment to authentic interpersonal relations, Law creates the conditions for their realization. From *Weltalter* onward, however, Schelling no longer accepts this notion of a possible reconciliation of Law and love: his notion of reconciliation now involves the act of passing beyond the domain of Law; as such, it seems close to the notion of "love beyond law" mentioned by Lacan in the very last page of *Seminar XI*.[85] It is indeed tempting to approach Schelling's reconciliation beyond Law from the perspective of Lacan's notion of the "feminine" sublimatiom of drives into love: for the late Lacan, love is no longer merely a narcissistic (mis)recognition to be opposed to desire as the subject's "truth," but a unique case of direct asexual sublimation (integration into the order of the signifier) of drives, of their *jouissance,* in the guise of the asexual Thing (music, religion . . .) experienced in ecstatic surrender.[86] What one should bear in mind apropos of this love beyond Law, this direct asexual sublimation of drive, is that it is inherently nonsensical, beyond meaning: meaning can only take place within the (symbolic)

Law – the moment we trespass the domain of Law, meaning changes into enjoy-meant (*jouis-sense*).[87]

Insofar as, according to Lacan, at the conclusion of the psychoanalytic cure, the subject assumes drive beyond fantasy and beyond (the Law of) desire, this Schellingian problematic of reconciliation also compels us to confront the question of the conclusion of the cure in all its urgency. If we discard the discredited standard formulas ("reintegration into the sociosymbolic space," etc.), only two options remain open: *desire* or *drive*. That is to say, either we conceive the conclusion of the cure as the assertion of the subject's radical openness to the enigma of the Other's desire no longer veiled by fantasmatic formations, or we risk the step beyond desire itself and adopt the position of the saint who is no longer bothered by the Other's desire as its decentered cause. In the case of the saint, the subject, in an unheard-of way, "causes itself," becomes its own cause: its cause is no longer decentered; that is, the enigma of the Other's desire no longer has any hold over it. How are we to understand this strange reversal? In principle, things are clear enough: by way of positing itself as its own cause, the subject fully assumes the fact that the object-cause of its desire is not a cause that precedes its effects but is retroactively posited by the network of its effects: an event is never simply in itself traumatic, it only becomes a trauma retroactively, by being "secreted" from the subject's symbolic space as its inassimilable point of reference. In this precise sense, the subject "causes itself" by way of retroactively positing that X which acts as the object-cause of its desire. This loop is constitutive of the subject; that is, an entity that does not "cause itself" is precisely not a subject but an object.[88] However, one should avoid conceiving this assumption as a kind of symbolic integration of the decentered Real, whereby the subject "symbolizes," assumes as an act of its free choice, the imposed trauma of the contingent encounter of the Real. One should always bear in mind that the status of the subject as such is hysterical: the subject "is" only through its confrontation with the enigma of *Che vuoi?* ("What do you want?") insofar as the Other's desire remains impenetrable, insofar as the subject doesn't know what object it is for the Other. Suspending this decentering of the cause is thus strictly equivalent to what Lacan called "subjective destitution," to the dehystericization by means of which the subject loses its status of subject.

The most elementary matrix of fantasy, of its temporal loop, is that of the "impossible" gaze by means of which the subject is present at the act of his/her own conception. What is at stake in it is the enigma of the Other's desire: by means of the fantasy formation, the subject provides an answer to "What am I for my parents, for their desire?" and thus endeavors to arrive at the "deeper meaning" of his or her existence, to discern the Fate involved in it – the reassuring lesson of fantasy is that "I was brought about with a special purpose."[89] Consequently, when at the end of the psychoanalytic cure I "traverse my fundamental fantasy," the point of it is not that, instead of being bothered by the enigma of the Other's desire, of what I am for others, I "subjectivize" my fate in the sense of its symbolization, of recognizing myself in a symbolic network or narrative for which I am fully responsible, but rather that I *fully assume the uttermost contingency of my being.* The subject becomes "cause of myself" in the sense of no longer looking for a guarantee of his or her existence in another's desire. One cannot overestimate the radical character of this move of Lacan: Lacan abandons here what is usually considered the very core of his teaching, the notion of the irreducibly "decentered" subject, the subject whose very emergence is grounded in the relationship to a constitutive alterity.

Another way to put it is to say that "subjective destitution" changes the register from desire to drive. Desire is historical and subjectivized, always and by definition unsatisfied, metonymical, shifting from one object to another since I do not actually desire what I want. What I actually desire is to sustain desire itself, to postpone the dreaded moment of its satisfaction. Drive, on the other hand, involves a kind of inert satisfaction that always finds its way; drive is nonsubjectivized ("acephalous"). Perhaps its paradigmatic expressions are the repulsive private rituals (sniffing at one's own sweat, sticking one's finger into one's nose . . .) that bring us intense satisfaction without us being aware of it, or, insofar as we are aware of it, without us being able to do anything about it, to prevent it. In Andersen's fairy tale "The Red Shoes," an impoverished young woman puts on a pair of magical shoes and almost dies when her feet won't stop dancing; she is saved only when an executioner cuts off her feet with his ax. Her still-shod feet dance on, whereas she is given wooden feet and finds peace in religion . . . These shoes stand for drive at its purest: an "undead" partial object that functions as a kind of impersonal willing – "it wants," it persists in its repetitive movement (of dancing), it follows its path and exacts its satisfaction at any price, irrespective of the subject's well-being.[90] This drive is that which is "in the subject more than herself": although the subject cannot ever "subjectivize" it, assume it as "her own" by way of saying "It is *me* who wants to do this!" it nonetheless operates in her very kernel.[91] Lacan's wager is that it is possible to *sublimate* this dull satisfaction – this is what, ultimately, art and religion are about.

Although there is no intersubjectivity proper in drive, drive nonetheless involves its own mode of relating to otherness: desire addresses itself to the symbolic big Other, it seeks active recognition from it, while drive addresses itself to the *silence* in the Other. The Other is here reduced to a silent witness, to a mute presence that endorses the subject's *jouissance* by way of emitting a silent sign of acknowledgment, a "Yes!" to drive. In order to exemplify this status of the Other in drive, let's not be afraid to reach for the lowest of the low – *Lassie Comes Home*. At the very end of the film, the wounded and tired dog proceeds along the streets of the small town toward the school in order to be there when classes end for her master, the young boy; on her way, she passes the workshop of the local blacksmith; when the blacksmith, an old bearded man, catches sight of the blood-stained animal approaching the school exactly on time, he silently nods in agreement. This silent nod is a Yes! to the Real of the drive, to the dog's uncompromising drive "always to return to her place" (see Lacan's definition of the Real as "that which always returns to its place"). And, perhaps, therein resides also the last gesture of the psychoanalyst announcing the conclusion of the cure: in such a silent Yes! – in a pure gesture of acknowledging that the analysand has traversed her/his fantasy, that she/he has reached beyond the enigma of *Che vuoi?* and turned into a being of drive.

Or, to put it in yet another way: desire as the desire of the Other remains within the domain of transference and the (big) Other; the ultimate experience is here that of anxiety, that is, the experience of the opaque trauma of the Other's desire, of what does the Other want from me (*Che vuoi?*). Drive, on the contrary, is outside transference and the reference to the Other (for that reason, the dissolution of transference equals the passage from desire to drive: there is no desire without transference). At the level of desire, the encounter with the Real occurs as the encounter of the Other's desire; at the level of drive, the Real is directly drive itself. Or, to put it in yet another way: desire is the desire of the Other, while drive is never the drive of the Other. With respect to literary references, this move "beyond desire" (to drive) is also a move *beyond Kafka:* the work of Kafka probably gives body to the experience of *Che vuoi?* – of the enigma of the impenetrable desire of the Other – at its most extreme, while drive involves the suspension of the dimension of the Other's desire. The Other who says "Yes!" to drive is not the Other of *Che vuoi?*[92]

Another way to formulate the opposition between desire and drive is to say that desire stands to interpretation as drive to sublimation: the fact that sublimation is as a rule mentioned apropos of drive, not of desire (Freud himself never speaks of the "sublimation of desire"), while, on the other hand, one also never speaks of the "interpretation of drive" but always links interpretation to desire, bears witness to a profound theoretical necessity. The title of Lacan's seminar from 1958–59, "Desire and Its Interpretation," is to be taken as a direct assertion of their ultimate identity: desire *coincides* with its own interpretation. That is, when the subject endeavors to interpret (its or, originally, the Other's) desire and never finds the ultimate point of reference, when it forever slides from one to another reading, this very desperate attempt to arrive at "what one really wants" is desire itself. (Or, to put it in a more elaborate way: insofar as the coordinates of desire are provided by the "fundamental fantasy," and insofar as this fantasy emerges as an attempt to provide an answer to the enigma of *Che vuoi?*, of the Other's desire – in short: as the interpretation of this desire, of what the Other "effectively wants from me" – desire as such is sustained by interpretation.) In a strictly homologous way, drive *is* its sublimation: there is no "direct" drive that is afterward sublimated, since the "nonsublimated drive" is simply the biological instinct: *drive* designates the moment when an instinct is "sublimated" – cut off from its natural point of satisfaction and attached to an object that acts as the stand-in for the impossible Thing – and, as such, condemned to the repetitive movement of encircling, never directly "swallowing," its object.[93]

A key moment in the recent e-mail discussion between Judith Butler and Ernesto Laclau about the relationship between failure and repetition (or iterability, to use the Derridean term) directly concerns this problematic of drive. The stakes of this discussion were high, since they directly concerned the alternative "Lacan or Hegel." That is to say, Butler claims that "the failure of any subject formation is an effect of its iterability, its having been formed in time, again and again. One might say, via Althusser, that the ritual through which subjects are formed is always subject to a rerouting or a lapse by virtue of this necessity to repeat and reinstall itself." Her point is clearly anti-Lacanian: if we accept the primacy of failure over repetition – that is, if we claim that repetition itself is driven by the failure of the subject to achieve its full self-identity – then we elevate, in a kind of negative foundational gesture, the failure (or lack) itself into the ultimate ontological universal condition: lack itself becomes a kind of common a priori shared by all ontic entities on account of their very failure to achieve full identity. (It was, of course, already Derrida who, in his "Le facteur de la vérité," accused Lacan of ontologizing the lack.) However, Butler's background is here more Nietzschean: repetition stands for the assertive movement of "return of the same," for the *excess* of the will that is not grounded in any prior lack. When, in his final response, Laclau emphasizes the ambiguity of Butler's statement that failure is an effect of iterability, his critical point is that giving preference to iterability over failure can bring us to (mis)perceive the process of repetition as a kind of Hegelian movement of *Aufhebung* in which particular failures are progressively sublated by way of their iteration – if there is no original lack opening up the space of repetition, if there is no lack that dislocates the entire series, then we obtain the radical immanence of the totality of the process to itself. The only thing that can prevent this dialectical closure is thus the assertion of a constitutive failure, of an ultimate deadlock. It is easy to miss the finesse of Laclau's point here: he not only claims that we must assert the gap between the ontological level of lack, of the impossible universal, and the repetitive endeavors of particular contents to hegemonize the universal; he also adds that, *precisely because this lack is irreducible,* there is always some particular content that hegemonizes the universal; that is, the relationship between universal and particular is always "pathologically" twisted on account of a short circuit between the two. We never reach the balance of the dialectical totality in which the Universal coincides with the plurality of its particular content, with the movement of mediation from one to the other particular moment driven by the failure of each particular moment to embody directly the universal totality. Laclau's implicit corrective to Hegel is that not only does no particular moment directly encompass the universal, the movement of mediation from one to another particular moment driven by the failure of each of them also does not do the job. What one should do here – apart from pointing out that Laclau's notion of dialectical totality perhaps simplifies Hegel's position and misses the way impossibility is cosubstantial to the Hegelian totality – is to point out how a kind of iterability that *precedes* the logic of lack is also central to Lacan, to his notion of drive as opposed to desire. The ambiguity of the relationship between failure and iterability mentioned by Laclau involves the very line of separation between desire and drive: insofar as lack precedes repetition and serves as its mobile, we are within the space of *desire,* whereas *drive* designates a repetitive movement not driven by a constitutive lack.

We can see, now, how we are to interpret the opposition between desire and drive. Insofar as desire remains our horizon, our position ultimately amounts to a kind of Levinasian openness to the enigma of the Other, to the imponderable mystery of the Other's desire. In a clear contrast to this attitude of respect for the Other in its transcendence, drive introduces radical immanence: desire is open to the transcendence of the Other, while drive is "closed," absolutely immanent. Or, to put it in a slightly different way, desire and drive are to be contrasted as subject and object: there is a *subject of desire* and an *object of drive*. In desire, the subject longs for the (lost) object, whereas in drive, the subject makes herself an object (the scopic drive, for example, involves an attitude of *se faire voir,* of "making-oneself-seen," not simply of wanting to see). Perhaps this is how we are to read Schelling's notion of the highest freedom as the state in which activity and passivity, being active and being acted upon, harmoniously overlap: humanity reaches this acme when it turns its very subjectivity into the Predicate of an ever higher Power (in the mathematical sense of the term), that is, when it, as it were, yields to the Other, "depersonalizes" its most intense activity and performs it as if some other, higher Power is acting through human beings, using them as its medium – like the mystical experience of Love, or like artists who, in the highest frenzy of creativity, experiences themselves as mediums through which some more substantial, impersonal Power expresses itself. The crucial point is to distinguish this position from that of a pervert who also undergoes a kind of "subjective destitution" and posits himself as the object-cause of the Other's desire (see the case of the Stalinist Communist who conceives himself as the pure object-instrument of the realization of the Necessity of History): for the pervert, the big Other exists, while the subject at the end of the psychoanalytic process assumes the *nonexistence* of the big Other. In short, the Other for whom the subject "makes herself . . . (seen, heard, active)" has no independent existence and ultimately relies on the subject herself – in this precise sense, the subject who makes herself the Other's object-cause *becomes her own cause.* In order to render this position of pure drive beyond the search for (symbolic) recognition, one is tempted to refer to Ayn Rand's *The Fountainhead,* a novel that is usually decried as the exemplary case of protofascist capitalist individualism. There is nonetheless a trace of authenticity in Rand's description of the momentary impact the architect Howard Roark, the hero of the novel, makes on the members of the audience in the courtroom where he stands trial:

> Roark took the oath. He stood by the steps of the witness stand. The audience looked at him. They felt he had no chance. They

could drop the nameless resentment, the sense of insecurity which he aroused in most people. And so, for the first time, they could see him as he was: a man totally innocent of fear.

The fear of which they thought was not the normal kind, not a response to a tangible danger, but the chronic, unconfessed fear in which they all lived. They remembered the misery of the moments when, in loneliness, a man thinks of the bright words he could have said, but had not found, and hates those who robbed him of his courage. The misery of knowing how strong and able one is in one's own mind, the radiant picture never to be made real. Dreams? Self-delusion? Or a murdered reality, unborn, killed by that corroding emotion without name – fear – need – dependence – hatred?

Roark stood before them as each man stands in the innocence of his own mind. But Roark stood like that before a hostile crowd – and they knew suddenly that no hatred was possible to him. For the flash of an instant, they grasped the manner of his consciousness. Each asked himself: do I need anyone's approval? – does it matter? – am I tied? And for that instant, each man was free – free enough to feel benevolence for every other man in the room.

It was only a moment; the moment of silence when Roark was about to speak.[94]

Indeed, as Lacan put it: a true Master is the one who cannot ever be betrayed – the one who, even when actually betrayed, does not lose anything. One can somewhat clarify this paradox through reference to Kant. As we have already seen, Kant is well aware that the condition of impossibility of our ethical activity is at the same time its condition of possibility: humanity's limitation to finitude, that is, the very condition that prevents it from fulfilling its ethical destination, is, at the same time, a positive condition of its ethical activity. For that reason, Kant holds sainthood not only to be impossible, unattainable in our terrestrial existence, but, at a more profound level, *undesirable:* moral consciousness is horrified at its prospect, since this state would close the gap that keeps the space for ethical activity open. This closing of the gap, however, is precisely what takes place at the conclusion of the cure: let us imagine, in the most naive terms, a direct access to the Absolute that suffocates the openness of desire: all of a sudden, "everything becomes clear," there is no longer any enigmatic X to sustain our desire – no wonder that the conclusion of the cure often involves the danger of a psychotic breakdown, or, at least, of severe depression . . . When Lacan conceives the conclusion of the cure as the moment when the subject, by way of its own destitution, changes into a "being of drive" and becomes its own cause, does this, then, not point towards the Schellingian Reconciliation?

A BIBLIOGRAPHICAL NOTE

The third draft of *Weltalter* was translated into English as *Schelling: The Ages of the World* (1813), translated by Frederick de Wolfe Bolman, Jr. (New York: Columbia University Press, 1942; reprint New York: AMS Press, 1967). In the recent profusion of books on Schelling, let us limit ourselves to ten studies; first, three German readings that provided the basic coordinates for the subsequent interpretations.

1. Martin Heidegger, *Schelling's Treatise on the Essence of Human Freedom* (Athens: Ohio University Press, 1985) (lectures presented in 1936). Heidegger's emphasis is on the inherent tension of Schelling's text between the German Idealist problematic of the System and Schelling's notion of freedom, which already points toward a post-idealist, even postmetaphysical, dimension of finitude and temporality.

2. Jürgen Habermas, "Dialektischer Idealismus im Übergang zum Materialismus – Geschichtsphilosophische Folgerungen aus Schellings Idee einer Contraction Gottes," in *Theorie und Praxis* (Berlin: Luchterhand, 1969), pp. 108–61 (left out of the English translation of *Theory and Practice!*). The first "progressive" appropriation of Schelling that interprets *Weltalter* as a break with the German Idealist logic of the Absolute, introducing the motif of radical historicity and contingency, and emphasizes the revolutionary political implications of this break.

3. Walter Schulz, *Die Vollendung des Deutschen Idealismus in der Spätphilosophie Schellings* (Pfullingen: Neske, 1975). A counterpoint to Habermas, a reading that insists that Schelling merely brought to

its conclusion the inherent logic of development of German Idealism.

TWO FRENCH STANDARD INTRODUCTIONS:

4. Xavier Tillette, *Schelling. Une philosophie en devenir* (Paris: Vrin, 1970). In the French tradition of the historical reconstructions of great philosophical systems à la Martial Gueroult, the standard reference work, full of erudition but with a shade of academic grayness.

5. Jean-Francois Marquet, *Liberté et existence. Etude sur la formation de la philosophie de Schelling* (Paris: Gallimard 1973). Probably *the* book on the development of Schelling's philosophy, with great attention to the fundamental deadlock Schelling again and again endeavored to resolve.

TWO RECENT ENGLISH INTRODUCTIONS:

6. Andrew Bowie, *Schelling and Modern European Philosophy: An Introduction* (London: Routledge, 1993). Arguably the best English-language introduction to Schelling, very good not only in providing a clear picture of the different stages of Schelling's philosophy, but also in displaying how Schelling announced a multitude of contemporary trends, from psychoanalysis to "deconstruction."

7. Edward Allen Beach, *The Potencies of God(s): Schelling's Philosophy of Mythology* (Albany; SUNY Press, 1994). A detailed examination of late Schelling's attempt to interpret the entire history of mythology as the imaginative expression of the elementary "potencies" (or powers) of the Absolute.

FINALLY, THREE "STRONG" INTERPRETATIONS:

8. Manfred Frank, *Der unendliche Mangel an Sein: Schellings Hegelkritik und die Anfänge der Marxschen Dialektik* (Frankfurt: Suhrkamp, 1975). Frank is most deserving for the reactualization of Schelling in the last two decades; this book, his first on Schelling, demonstrates the roots of Marxism as well as Sartrean Existentialism in the late Schelling's turn against Hegel.

9. Wolfram Hogrebe, *Prädikation und Genesis* (Frankfurt: Suhrkamp, 1989). An extremely refined approach to *Weltalter* from the problematic of discursivity, focused on the passage from the pre-

discursive rotary motion of drives to the articulated universe of the Word.

10. Slavoj Žižek, *The Indivisible Remainder: An Essay on Schelling and Related Matters* (London: Verso, 1996). A Lacanian reading of "Philosophical Investigations into the Essence of Human Freedom" and *Weltalter,* listed here simply because it provides a more exhaustive development of the themes outlined in this introduction.

NOTES

1. F. W. J. Schelling, *Grundlegung der positiven Philosophie* (Torino, 1972), p. 222 (quoted from Wolfram Hogrebe, *Prädikation und Genesis* [Frankfurt: Suhrkamp, 1989], p. 39).

2. F. W. J. Schelling, *Sämtliche Werke,* ed. K. F. A. Schelling (Stuttgart: Cotta, 1856–61).

3. F. W. J. Schelling, *Die Weltalter. Fragmente. In den Urfassungen von 1811 und 1813,* ed. Manfred Schroeter (Munich: Biederstein 1946).

4. "Plato's secret teaching" also offers an example of how the role of the initiatory secret doctrine is to patch the lack in the big Other (the field of Knowledge), its inconsistency. That is to say, the main argument for the existence of Plato's secret teaching is the negative-dialectic character of the majority of Plato's dialogues, from the earlier Socratic ones to *Parmenides:* these dialogues undermine *a doxa* without supplying a positive teaching to replace it – what (philosophical) common sense finds unacceptable is that the big Other's inconsistency comes first and that the secret teaching is a secondary fantasmatic restitution of the unmutilated wholeness of the doctrine.

5. See F. W. J. Schelling, "Philosophical Investigations into the Essence of Human Freedom and Related Matters," in *Philosophy of German Idealism,* ed. Ernst Behler (New York: Continuum, 1987).

6. See Jacques Derrida, "Cogito and the History of Madness," in *Writing and Difference* (Chicago: University of Chicago Press, 1978).

7. Quoted from Donald Phillip Verene, *Hegel's Recollection* (Albany: SUNY Press, 1985, pp. 7–8).

8. Ibid., p. 8.

9. See Jean-Pierre Dupuy, *Le sacrifice et l'envie* (Paris: Calman-Levy, 1992).

10. Far from being a surplus that comes after our profane needs are satisfied, the Sacred is thus at the beginning; that is, the story *begins* with an excessive expenditure and only then passes to its economization, to rational calculation of needs, or, as Schelling put it, the Beginning is the negation of the process, of what begins with it. For that

reason, the enlightened perspective that takes as its starting point the priority of real needs and wonders at superfluous expenditure while so many basic needs remain unsatisfied, is misleading. A brief reminder from the history of early capitalism is very instructive as to this point: automatic machines were first developed as a surplus, as toys intended to amuse the king's gaze (the famous machines in the garden of Versailles); it was only afterward that they were put to real use and applied to increase productivity.

11. Schelling, *Die Weltalter,* p. 134; see the translation in the present volume, p. 132. (Hereafter, page references to the present translation will be given in square brackets.) Significantly, Schelling resorts to the same formulation when, in his *Letters on Dogmatism and Criticism,* he describes the falsehood of a person entertaining the notion of his own death: when indulging in fantasies about one's own death, one always imagines oneself as miraculously surviving one's death and being present at the scene of one's own funeral in the guise of a pure gaze that observes the universe from which one is already absent, relishing the imagined pathetic reactions of the relatives, etc. We are thereby at the fundamental time-loop of fantasy: to be present as a pure gaze prior to one's own conception or decease. Is therefore the God prior to the primordial contraction, this pure gaze that finds enjoyment in contemplating its own nonbeing, also not a fantasy formation at its purest? Schelling emphasizes again and again that the passage of the pure *Seinkoennen* of the primordial Abyss into the contracted Ground cannot be accounted for or deduced: it can only be described (narrated) *post festum,* after it already took place, since we are not dealing with a necessary act but with a free act that could also not have happened – however, does this not amount to an implicit admission of the fact that its status is that of a retroactive fantasy?

12. Ibid., p. 13.

13. Schelling, *Sämtliche Werke,* 8:43.

14. Ibid., p. 715.

15. Ibid., p. 712.

16. See Hogrebe, *Prädikation und Genesis,* p. 100.

17. On a somewhat different level, the "loss of reality" entailed by the too close correspondence of words with things is also the theme of the greatly underrated *Leap of Faith,* a story of a manipulative and

utterly cynical preacher (Steve Martin) who earns his money amusing small-town farmers by faked miracle healings performed in a circus tent; when the younger brother of a local waitress he wants to seduce asks him to heal his crippled legs and make him walk again, he openly tells the boy that his performance is a fraud; the boy continues to believe in him and approaches him with the same demand in a crowded tent; unable to avoid the challenge, the hero goes through his usual motions, with an eye to a possible escape route; however, this time, his "healing" miraculously works, and this encounter with the real, the unexpected success of his performance, is what thoroughly devastates the hero – he escapes the town, abandoning forever the life of a preacher.

18. See Diana Fuss, *Identification Papers,* (New York: Routledge, 1995).

19. See Jacqueline Rose, "Negativity in the Work of Melanie Klein," in *Why War?* (Oxford: Blackwell, 1993), pp. 167–68. A homologous concept of contradiction was elaborated by Etienne Balibar apropos of Spinoza. See Etienne Balibar, "Spinoza, the Anti-Orwell: The Fear of the Masses," in *Masses, Classes, Ideas* (New York: Routledge, 1994).

20. We rely here on Mark Cousins's excellent "The Ugly," in *AA Files* nos. 28, 29 (London, 1994).

21. Impossible not to recall here Swift's description of how Gulliver experienced the gigantic body of a beautiful woman at Brobdingnag: "no object ever disgusted me so much as the sight of her monstrous breast . . . so varified with spots, pimples and freckles, that nothing could appear more nauseous." On the other hand, one should also bear in mind the opposite procedure: when one approaches the disgusting wiggling of life even further and gets absolutely close to it, it is no longer perceived as alive but assumes abstract forms – it is well known that microcosms (atoms, molecules), at least the way we visualize them, uncannily resemble macrocosms (planets in their orbits). When we approach matter "absolutely," it loses its density and dissolves into the undulation of abstract patterns. We have thus four levels: the abstract planetary macrocosm; ordinary reality; the Real of the "ugly life-substance"; and, again, the abstract planetary microcosm.

22. See chapter 4 of Slavoj Žižek, *Enjoy Your Symptom!* (New York: Routledge, 1992).

23. See chapter 5 of Slavoj Žižek, *Metastases of Enjoyment* (London: Verso, 1994).

24. In this precise sense, the title of Bernard Baas's standard essay on Kant and Lacan – "Le desir pur" – is fully justified; see Bernard Bass, "Le desir pur," in *Ornicar?* 38 (Paris: Navarin, 1986).

25. Walter Benn Michaels, "Race and Culture," *Critical Inquiry* (summer 1992): 682–85.

26. For a more detailed account of this real kernel of ethnic identity, see chapter 6 of Slavoj Žižek, *Tarrying with the Negative* (Durham: Duke University Press, 1993).

27. See Jacques Ranciere, *On the Shores of Politics* (London: Verso, 1995), p. 22.

28. Fredric Jameson, *The Seeds of Time* (New York: Columbia University Press, 1994), pp. 43–44.

29. A further example of such hasty correlations is provided by the commonplace according to which man stands toward woman as desire toward drive, as dynamic, self-transgressing movement against circular, repetitive inertia. However, is the inverted correlation not equally defensible – the hysterical woman as the embodiment of desire against the reliability of man's drive? The political overdetermination of the first commonplace is obvious: drive is reactionary and desire revolutionary; i.e., desire designates the dynamic force of subversion and change, while drive stands for the repetitive inertia of a closed circular movement. Is then the late Lacan who elevates drive over desire conservative? Is, however, the notion of drive as that which insists in its subterranean work of slowly undermining resistance not also the best exemplification of the logic of the revolutionary process?

30. The category of vanishing mediator was introduced by Fredric Jameson apropos of Max Weber (see "The Vanishing Mediator; or, Max Weber as Storyteller," in *The Ideologies of Theory* vol. 2 [Minneapolis: University of Minnesota Press, 1988]).

31. Is not the best argument for this gap, for this relative independence of the political from the libidinal, the fact that we witness today the flourishing of rightist as well as leftist and even centrist paranoiac conspiracy theories?

32. Schelling, *Die Weltalter,* pp. 183–84 [179–80].

33. See Jean-Francois Marquet, *Liberté et existence. Etude sur la formation de la philosophie de Schelling* (Paris: Gallimard, 1973).

34. Ibid., p. 464.

35. Ibid., pp. 541–42.

36. Narrativization as such is an elementary ideological gesture, from the primitive myths that explain "the origins of . . ." to the capitalist narrative of primordial accumulation. Fredric Jameson's well-known assertion that "the production of aesthetic or narrative form is to be seen as an ideological act in its own right, with the function of inventing imaginary or formal solutions to unresolvable social contradictions"(Fredric Jameson, *The Political Unconscious* [Ithaca: Cornell University Press, 1981] p. 79), applies perfectly to Schelling's *Weltalter:* in order to resolve the contradiction of Absolute Idealism and its procedure of logical deduction, or, more precisely, to avoid its materialist resolution, he resorts to the form of a philosophico-mythological narrative.

37. One can see now why Schelling's philosophy is incompatible with the New Age attitude of Wisdom: wisdom is profound, i.e., it comes *from below,* from the depth of the eternal rotary motion (wisdom expresses itself in statements like "everything that is born must die," "the wheel of fortune is turning all the time," etc.), whereas Schelling's endeavor is precisely to break this rotary motion and gain access to the domain of Word that intervenes *from above.*

38. This unhistorical gap that keeps open the space for historicization also allows us to account for the difference between the standard symbolic narrative and the fantasmatic narrative: the standard symbolic narrative remains within the space of historicization, whereas the fantasmatic narrative (of the primordial loss, castration) endeavors to tell the story of the emergence of the gap of historicization itself, of how the gap (the loss) itself took place.

39. Schelling, *Die Weltalter,* pp. 56–57.

40. See "Stuttgart Seminars," in *Idealism and the Endgame of Theory: Three Essays by F. W. J. Schelling* (Albany: SUNY Press, 1994).

41. F. W. J. Schelling, *On the History of Modern Philosophy* (Cambridge: Cambridge University Press, 1994), p. 115.

42. Ibid.

43. Ibid., p. 116.

44. Ibid.

45. See Jon Elster, *Sour Grapes* (Cambridge: Cambridge University Press, 1982).

46. Schelling, *History of Modern Philosophy*, p. 115.

47. See Hogrebe, *Prädikation und Genesis*, pp. 102–3.

48. Schelling, *Sämtliche Werke*, 8:629.

49. See Daniel Breazeadale, "Check or Checkmate? On the Finitude of the Fichtean Self," in *The Modern Subject: Conceptions of the Self in Classical German Philosophy,* ed. Karl Ameriks and Dieter Sturma (Albany: SUNY Press, 1995), pp. 87–114.

50. Ibid., p. 100.

51. What imposes itself here is the parallel between the Fichtean *Anstoss* and the Freudian-Lacanian scheme of the relationship between the primordial *Ich (Ur-Ich)* and the object, the foreign body in its midst, which disturbs its narcissistic balance, setting in motion the long process of the gradual expulsion and structuration of this inner snag through which (what we experience as) "external, objective reality" is constituted (see chap. 3 of Žižek, *Enjoy Your Symptom!*).

52. With regard to paternal authority, "no Spirit without Spirits" reads "no symbolic paternal function without the obscene figure of Father-Enjoyment"; as to this duality, see Slavoj Žižek, "'I Hear You with My Eyes'; or, The Invisible Master," in *Voice and Gaze as Love Object,* Renata Salecl and Slavoj Žižek (Durham: Duke University Press, 1996). When, in part 2 of Shakespeare's *Henry IV,* after Prince Hal's coronation, Falstaff approaches his former accomplice in merrymaking, the new king rebuffs him with the words that render nicely the unreal, dream like, quality of this other obscene paternal figure: "How ill white hairs become a fool and jester! / I have long dream'd of such a kind of man, / So surfeit-swell'd, so old, and so profane, / But, being awak'd, I do despise my dream"(5.5.52–55).

53. Apropos of this material weight of van Gogh paintings, one can articulate the difference between traditional and modern painting: in the traditional painting, the stain is limited, located to the anamorphic element (the protracted-distorted skull in *Ambassadors,* etc.), whereas in van Gogh, the stain in a way spreads over, pervades the entire painting, so that every element within the frame is a depiction of some "real object" and simultaneously a stain with its proper material weight.

54. It was already Henry James who was well aware that there is silence and silence – in his *Transatlantic Sketches* from 1875, he pro-

vided a nice description of the difference between the silence of the canals in Venice and in Amsterdam: "In the one it is the stillness of order, and in the other of vacancy – the sleep of idleness and the sleep of rest; the quiet that comes of letting everything go by the board, and the quiet that comes of doing things betimes and being able to sit with folded hands and say they are well done."

55. This means that, at the same time, this universal frame is never effectively empty, i.e., that it is *always-already* occupied, filled in, by some contingent content. The ideological illusion of Richard Rorty, exemplary of political liberalism, resides in his belief that it is possible to draw a clear line of separation between the universal-neutral frame and the multitude of particular contents, i.e., to establish a society within which a universal frame of neutral rules would guarantee the coexistence of the multitude of "private worlds," of individuals and/or groups pursuing their particular interests: what gets lost here is the fundamental lesson of the logic of hegemony according to which this universal frame is the battleground where particular contents fight for predominance. Does Rorty not accomplish here a move that is strictly homologous to ego psychology? The latter asserts a conflict-free sphere of the ego not caught in libidinal conflicts and deadlocks of repression, able to reason in a neutral, rational way, the same as Rorty, who asserts the possibility of establishing a conflict-free sphere of neutral social rules not caught in the deadlock of particular fantasies.

56. Today's *multiculturalist* ideology provides an exemplary case of the falsity of a direct universalist position: multiculturalism is clearly a disavowed, inverted, form of racism, a "racism with a distance" – it respects the Other's identity, conceiving the Other as a self-enclosed authentic community toward which the multiculturalist maintains a distance rendered possible by his or her privileged universal position. In other words, multiculturalism is a racism that empties its own position of all positive content (the multiculturalist is not a direct racist, he or she does not oppose to the Other the particular values of his own culture), but nonetheless retains this position as the privileged empty point of universality from which one is able to appreciate properly other particular cultures – the multiculturalist's respect for the Other's specificity is the very form of asserting one's own superiority.

57. We rely here on Ernesto Laclau and Lilian Zac, "Minding the Gap: The Subject of Politics," in *The Making of Political Identities,* ed. Ernesto Laclau (London: Verso, 1994).

58. We also find an echo of the same paradoxical structure in the hero's encounter with his evil opponent in fairy tales. As is well known from Propp's morphology of fairy tales, this encounter as a rule occurs twice: first, there is the opponent's sudden, surprising entry from aside, perturbing the hero's progress; then, at the end of the story, the hero (who, after the first encounter, gets involved in a long search for the evil opponent) finally locates him in some central mysterious place and fights him. What we have here are the two modalities of the encounter of the Real: a sudden intrusion from aside and the central point that eludes our grasp – the Real is that which eludes our grasp and, simultaneously, that which intrudes, imposes its presence on us, when least expected.

59. We rely here on Bruce Fink, *The Lacanian Subject* (Princeton: Princeton University Press, 1995), especially p. 65.

60. As a general rule, in the analysis of narrative works of art, one should focus on those places where the line of separation between reality and its fantasmatic supplement splits from within the narrative space. Alex Tarnopolsky, in his analysis of Verdi's *Rigoletto* ("Loss and Mourning in Verdi's *Rigoletto,*" *New Formations* 26, pp. 89–106), argues that the scene of Gilda's abduction from the end of act 1 clearly stages a dream – this is the only way to account for the fact that the spectator is ready to overlook its utterly improbable nature. In order to prove his case, Tarnopolsky translates this scene into the narrative of a dream "as Rigoletto might have reported it to his psychoanalyst, had he been a patient on a couch":

> A group of people in a remote street. They were all masked. It was dark. They discovered a rare beautiful woman but I could only have a glimpse of her. They think she is my mistress. They were planning to steal her. When I appeared, they hid. They told me that they were abducting someone else's wife. They blindfolded me and asked me to hold the ladder! They went up and down, noisily. When they left I discovered that they had taken my daughter. I stood there, paralysed, overwhelmed, cursing. (P. 102)

97

Some of the exemplary contemporary stagings of Wagner's operas seem to follow the same insight: in Ponelle's version of *Tristan*, for example, the events of the last half hour (Isolde's arrival and *Liebestod*) are presented as the hallucination of the dying Tristan, thus rendering visible the split at work in the texture of Wagner's opera itself.

61. A more detailed analysis should develop the obvious parallel between *The Crying Game* and Hitchcock's *Psycho* and *Vertigo,* two films whose narrative also takes an unexpected turn after the main character dies one-third into the film: Dil's game of masquerade is strictly homologous to Kim Novak's game between semblance (Madeleine) and truth (Judy).

62. Insofar as that which makes us fall in love is never the partner's perfection but always an "endearing foible," an index of her/his *imperfection,* one is tempted to say that this final revelation of Daphne's "imperfection" effectively seals the millionaire's love for "her."

63. One of the motifs often encountered in science fiction is that of a group of travelers who pass through a "stargate" into another spatial dimension (alternative universe, etc.); once they arrive there, something goes wrong, so that they are unable to return to their home and are forever stuck in the Other Space. However, is this not the situation of all of us, human mortals, dislocated, caught in a fantasmatic universe, condemned to a shadowy existence from which there is no escape?

64. James Naremore, *The Magic World of Orson Welles* (New York: Oxford University Press, 1978), pp. 248–49.

65. Ibid., p. 248.

66. At a somewhat different level, another sign of the same tendency is the fact that today, failures themselves have lost their Freudian subversive potential and are becoming more and more the topic of a show: one of the most popular shows on American TV is "The best bloopers of . . .," bringing together fragments of TV series, movies, news, etc., that were censored because something stupid occurred (the actor confused his lines, slipped up . . .). From time to time, one even gets the impression that the slips themselves are carefully planned so that they can be used in a show about the making of the show. The best indicator of this devaluation of the slip is the

use of the term "Freudian slip" ("O, I just made a Freudian slip!") that totally suspends its subversive sting.

67. Deleuze's example is the "event" of the breakdown of the splendor of the Roaring Twenties in F. Scott Fitzgerald's late novels; see Gilles Deleuze, *La logique du sens* (Paris: Editions de Minuit, 1967), pp. 180–81.

68. As to the distinction between imitation and simulation, see Benjamin Wooley, *Virtual Worlds* (Oxford: Blackwell, 1992).

69. Andrew Cutrofello's *The Owl at Dawn* (Albany: SUNY Press, 1995), a sequel to Hegel's *Phenomenology of Spirit* covering the period from Hegel's death to today, closely imitates the structure of Hegel's "original" as well as its style – so why does the reading of this book give rise to anxiety in a Hegelian (like myself)? What one is afraid of is not that Cutrofello will fail, but that he will *succeed* – why? One reads *The Owl at Dawn* as a pastiche, as an ironic imitation of Hegel's "original," so if it succeeds too well, this means that, in a sense, *the original itself is already a fake*, that its status is that of ironic imitation – the success of *The Owl at Dawn* retroactively denaturalizes the original.

70. See lecture 23 ("Psychoanalysis and Cybernetics") in *The Seminar of Jacques Lacan. Book II: The Ego in Freud's Theory and in the Technique of Psychoanalysis (1954–1955)* (New York: Norton, 1988).

71. See chapter 3 of Jacques Lacan, *Le seminaire, livre XX: Encore* (Paris: Editions du Seuil, 1975).

72. See Jacques Lacan, "Television," in *October* 40 (1987).

73. The main work of Nicolas Malebranche is *Recherches de la verité* (1674–75; the most available edition Paris: Vrin, 1975). In our reading of Malebranche, we rely on Miran Božovič, "Malebranchian Occasionalism; or, Philosophy in the Garden of Eden," *Filozofski Vestnik* 1 (Ljubljana: Slovene Academy of Sciences, 1995). Incidentally, occasionalism also enables us to throw new light on the exact status of the Fall: Adam was brought to ruin and banished from Paradise not because he was simply led astray by Eve's sensuality; the point is rather that he made a philosophical mistake and regressed from occasionalism to vulgar sensual empiricism according to which material objects directly, without the mediation of the big Other (God), affect our senses – *the Fall is primarily a question of Adam's philosophical convictions.* That is to say, prior to the Fall, Adam fully

mastered his body and maintained a distance toward it: since he was well aware that the connection between his soul and his body is contingent and only occasional, he was at any moment able to suspend it, to cut himself off and to feel neither pain nor pleasure. Pain and pleasure were not ends in themselves, they served only to provide information about what is bad or good for the survival of his body. The Fall occurred the moment Adam excessively (i.e., beyond the scope needed to provide the information necessary for survival in the natural environs) yielded to his senses, the moment his senses affected him to such an extent that he lost his distance toward them and was distracted from pure thought. The object responsible for the Fall, of course, was Eve: Adam fell when the view of Eve naked momentarily distracted him and led him astray into believing that Eve in herself, directly and not only occasionally, was the cause of his sexual pleasure – Eve is responsible for the Fall insofar as she gave rise to the philosophical error of sensual realism. When Lacan claims that *la femme n'existe pas,* one has to read this proposition as a decisive argument for occasionalism and against sensual empiricism: when a man sexually enjoys a woman, the woman is not a direct but only an occasional cause of his enjoyment; he enjoys a woman because God (the big Other, the symbolic network) sustains her as the object of satisfaction. In other words, *Eve* stands for the primordial fetishist disavowal of castration, of the fact that the effect of a sensual object (woman) is not directly grounded in its properties, but is mediated by its symbolic place. And, as was already pointed out by Saint Augustine, the punishment, the price Adam had to pay for his Fall, was, quite appropriately, that he was no longer able to master fully his body – the erection of his phallus escaped his control. If, then, the Fall involves a change in Adam's philosophical attitude, and, furthermore, if it is the Fall that creates Woman, that brings her into being – not at the ontic level, but as to her ontological status, as the temptress correlative to man's desire (things are thus even worse than Otto Weininger thought: as to her ontological status, Woman is the outcome of man's philosophical error) – what, if any at all, was the philosophical attitude of *Eve?*

74. As to this ambiguity, see Paul Virilio, *The Art of the Motor* (Minneapolis: University of Minnesota Press, 1995).

75. The notion of this connection between cyberspace and Schreber's psychotic universe was suggested to me by Wendy Chun, Princeton.

76. See part 1 ("The Antinomies of Postmodernity") of Jameson, *The Seeds of Time.*

77. There are two notions of Limit at work here: the Limit as the inherent form, the proper measure, which enables us to lead a balanced existence; the Limit as the asymptotic borderline that – if we come too close to it – causes a catastrophic disintegration of our universe.

78. The same paradox of superego is clearly discernible in the impasse of sexual harassment: there is no proper measure, no unambiguous line of demarcation separating the "correct" sexual flirting from "uncorrect" harassment. Sexual play as such is excessive, aggressive; i.e., the same act or feature that, from one perspective, is perceived as harassment, can, in different circumstances, turn the partner on. In short, one *has* to violate the rules (the PC rules as well as the macho rules of conquest). If one goes beyond the limit, one is either harassing or successfully flirting; if one stays below the limit, one is either perceived as a weakling or, again, successfully flirting – there is no metarule to guarantee the success or the correctness of our procedure. In other terms, the subject is caught between provocation and prohibition, between guilt and being wimpy: the other, the one you endeavor to seduce, is ambiguously provoking you to make a pass – if you dare do it, you are guilty, if you do not do it, you are a wimp.

79. Lacan provides the general matrix of this codependence between lack and excess in his (unpublished) seminar on Identification from 1961–62, by means of reference to the Kantian distinction between the empty notion without object and the object without notion: the barred subject as the void of negativity ($) is an empty notion without object, a hole in the (symbolic) structure, whereas the object small *a,* the cause of desire, is an excessive object without notion, a surplus over the notional structure, an inert remainder with no place in the structure. As such, these two elements are correlative: the surplus object functions as the placeholder of the subject's lack; i.e., the subject "encounters itself" among objects in the guise of a surplus that resists symbolization. For a more detailed account of it, see chapter 5 of Žižek, *Metastases of Enjoyment.*

80. Cinema executives obsessed with testing new films through special previews and then frantically reshooting new endings etc. fall victim to the homologous illusion: this utter adaptability to the whims of the public as a rule ends up in failure – what the public wants is a Master capable of *imposing* a version on it, not a pliable servant.

81. One is even tempted to risk a wild hypothesis and to claim that this gap has a physiological basis in the *double* climax of the orgasmic experience: first, there is the "point of no return" after which, for a couple of seconds, we "float in the bliss"; then, the ensuing second climax releases the tension. The cliché according to which Wagner's climactic moments (the finale of the overture to *Lohengrin*, the finale of *Tristan*) are "orgasmic" thus seems justified: here, also, the climactic moment is double; i.e., the first climax ends the restraint, sets free the forces, but does not yet release the tension – for that, another climax is needed.

82. During my stay at Princeton University as a Visiting Fellow, I was told that I could visit freely the dormitories' lounge and enjoy a free lunch or dinner – I would not have to pay, since the fact that I socialized with students and other faculty members was already considered a profit for the University. In short, when I visited the lounge and had lunch or dinner, the price I paid for it was that I visited the lounge and had lunch or dinner.

83. We are relying here on Jean-Michel Lasry, "Common Knowledge," in *Ornicar?* 28 (Paris: Navarin, 1982).

84. See chapters 1 and 6 of Mark Dery, *Escape Velocity: Cyberculture at the End of the Century* (New York: Grove Press, 1996).

85. See chapter 20 of Jacques Lacan, *The Four Fundamental Concepts of Psycho-Analysis* (New York: Norton, 1979).

86. See chapters 6 and 7 of Lacan, *Le seminaire, livre XX*. English translation: "God and the *Jouissance* of The Woman" / "A Love Letter," in Jacques Lacan and the *Ecole freudienne, Feminine Sexuality* (London: MacMillan, 1982).

87. It is at this point that Peter Dews's attempt to enlist Lacan, the Lacanian problematic of "love beyond Law," into his project of the "return to meaning" (see Peter Dews, *The Limits of Disenchantment* [London: Verso, 1996]) falls short: it has to overlook the radical incompatibility of "love beyond Law" and the field of meaning, i.e., the

fact that, within the Lacanian conceptual edifice, "love beyond Law" entails the eclipse of meaning in *jouis-sense.*

88. As to this paradoxical status of trauma, see chapter 2 of Žižek, *Metastases of Enjoyment.*

89. We can see, now, in what precise sense a pervert lives his fantasy: in clear contrast to the hysteric (neurotic), the pervert does not have any doubt as to what he is for the big Other's desire – he is the instrument of the Other's enjoyment. A simple, but nonetheless poignant, expression of this attitude of the pervert is found in Hugh Hudson's *Chariots of Fire,* when the devout Eric Liddel explains his fast running, which brought him a gold medal at the 1924 Paris Olympics: "God made me for a purpose, but He also made me fast. And when I run, I feel His pleasure."

90. Insofar as, for Lacan, drive as such is ultimately the death drive, the Freudian antagonism between Eros and Thanatos has to be transposed within the death drive itself. The death drive thus stands simultaneously for life that persists beyond (what Lacan calls the first, biological) death – the life of the undead – *and* for the endeavor to end up this very life-beyond-death. Eros designates the horrifying Real of the "love/life beyond death," of the immortal drive, while Thanatos stands for the striving to end this horror.

91. One should mention here Michael Powell's *The Red Shoes,* a suicidal variation of the same motif: at the end of the film, the shoes the young ballerina is wearing also take on a life of their own; however, since there is no one there to cut her legs off, the shoes carry the ballerina out onto a high balcony from which she is forced to leap onto the railway tracks and is hit by a train. The crucial thing this cinematic version adds to Andersen's fairy tale is the opposition between the "partial drive" embodied in the shoes and the normal sexual desire, i.e., the girl's sexual interest in her partner.

92. This also opens up two ways to interpret the passage from Jewish religion to Christianity: in the first, standard reading, Christian love obfuscates the anxiety of the Jewish enigma of the Other's desire (what does God want from me?), while in the second reading, Christian love points toward the dimension of drive beyond Law.

93. This difference between instinct and drive also overlaps with that between the two French terms for knowledge, *connaissance* and

savoir: instinct is an innate knowledge that tells the animal organism how to act (how to copulate, where to fly in winter, etc.), while humans lack such a knowledge and therefore have to rely on symbolic tradition (see Longinus's *Daphnis and Chloe,* in which the two lovers need to resort to the knowledge of elder, experienced people to learn how to copulate: relying on their instinct or imitating animals does not help much.).

94. Ayn Rand, *The Fountainhead* (New York: Signet, 1993), p. 677.

AGES OF THE WORLD

F. W. J. von Schelling

Translated by Judith Norman

Ages of the World:
Text and Context of the Translation

etween the years 1811 and 1815, Schelling made numerous
attempts to write a philosophical account of the nature of
time and creation. This text is a translation of the second
of three extant drafts of the work, which Schelling planned to call
Die Weltalter, the *Ages of the World.* All of the drafts are fragmen-
tary; Schelling barely got further than book I, which treated the
first "age of the world," the past. He would eventually abandon
the project.

Despite this rather inauspicious history, the text has considerable merit. Indeed, the very fact that Schelling could never resolve the difficulties inherent in the project is itself instructive,
giving insights into the pitfalls this trajectory of thought is likely
to encounter, while at the same time indicating the contours of
post-Idealist system philosophy. Žižek's essay is a powerful argument for the enduring interest and relevance of the work – in
short, for its modernity. I wish to add a few contextualizing remarks on the translation, and explanations of Schelling's termi-
nology, to insure that the merits of the text are not obscured by its
difficulties.

Throughout his intellectual development, Schelling was
broadly concerned with the philosophical problem of how conditioned, particular things arose out of a prior, absolutely unconditioned state. The emphasis in this question is on the *how,* asking
as to the manner in which finitude emerges and the relation it
bears to its unconditioned foundation. (A familiar, theological
form of this problem asks why a perfect God would create finite,
imperfect entities.) The issue bears a historic relation to the Kantian problem of how the empirical world arises out of a transcendental ground. Given that the unconditioned, foundational principle is self-caused or self-sufficient, there is no lack that it needs

to satisfy, and hence no sufficient reason (no ground) why it should give rise to something other than itself (viz., something grounded).

The *Ages of the World* treats a specific instance of the general problem of the emergence of particularity. It attempts to explain how time arose from eternity, or, more precisely, how something we call "the past" emerged as a specific dimension of time and came to ground the present. Clearly, this is not a historical question in any conventional sense; Schelling cannot presuppose temporality (and certainly not history), because it is precisely what he is trying to explain. Rather, he will give a general account of the state of things before creation, and attempt to show how the various forces at work in eternity could only achieve a stable configuration if placed in a relation of temporality. The bulk of the text is concerned with a description of the nature of eternity, the forces active within it, and the free act that resolves their tension by the stipulation of a temporal relationship. It is an act that Schelling identifies with divine creation. This is clearly not a creation *ex nihilo,* but rather a rearrangement of an extant state that Schelling identifies as "primal nature."

Of particular interest is Schelling's account of the production of the grounding relationship. He draws upon concepts that occupied him in his earlier writings on the philosophy of nature and argues that all development involves two basic forces (or wills): an attracting, enclosing, negative force and an expansive, outgoing, positive force. Schelling maintains that these forces are not distinct but are the same at some level. He suggests that the perennial problem of mind-body interaction might be solved by recognizing that the corporeal aspect of the individual is simply the negating side of the unity, and the spiritual aspect is the positive side. But Schelling further conceives the unity of the forces as the unity of ground and consequent. A negating, inward-drawing force must act as the ground of an expansive force. How can something act as a ground, unless it refuses expansion? Life begins with contraction, an envelopment that resists development. But this is only the beginning; life itself consists in a continual overcoming, a struggle against obstacles. It can only begin if an obstacle is placed at its ground, something to be continually overcome. The obstacle, moreover, must persist, or else the struggle that constitutes life would come to an end. Against a Hegelian notion that the beginning is sublated in development, Schelling argues that the ground must endure, and the act by which the ground is overcome must be a constant one as well.

This is all quite relevant to the topic at hand. In the text, Schelling refers to time as "an organism," a form of life that, like all forms of life, only develops by continually overcoming a resistant, unconscious ground – the past. It is a condition for all life that something be posited as past, as a ground for an expansive, loving presence. Schelling uses the terms *vorangehende* and *folgende* to describe the successive dimensions of time. The German terms have a greater ambiguity than the English; they mean logically "antecedent" and "consequent" states as well as temporally "preceding" and "succeeding" ones. Schelling makes good use of this ambiguity, demonstrating the relationship between the logical and chronological dimensions of the notion of grounding. Furthermore, Schelling describes the originary act through which the past is laid as the ground of the present as a free one, and the language of voluntarism dominates his discussion. The necessary course of time is thus freely produced, making present a manifest, comprehensible world.

This is a text of considerable scope and audacity. While Schelling admits that it is not the "great heroic poem" he thinks the material requires, it undoubtedly has an air of drama, which reaches a peak when discussing topics Schelling believes to be pushing the limits of human comprehension. Schelling is exploring ways to articulate structures that make articulacy possible in the first place, and describe events that preceded temporality itself. All this makes the text often quite baffling, particularly for the reader not familiar with specific developments in the German Idealist movement. A short glossary of some of the key terms might be of use.

Being (*das Seyn*) and what-is (or a thing-that-is) (*das Seyende*): Schelling uses the dichotomy between being and what-is to denote the opposing forces in all existence. We might (with some qualifications) associate the term *being* with the real, or, alternatively, with the notion of objectivity; *what-is* would then be paired with the ideal, or, alternatively, subjectivity. But it would be far more accurate to say that being and what-is relate to each other as real and ideal under certain circumstances. Schelling also discusses the being/what-is dichotomy in terms of negative and positive forces, where the negating force can, under certain circumstances, come to ground the positive force. It is essential to keep in mind that being and what-is are not separable; they are more like two aspects of the same thing.

This is a significant dichotomy for Schelling's discussion. He invokes it mainly to explain the two, opposing forces in eternity. In this context, Schelling sometimes refers to these opposites as "what-eternally-is" [*das ewige Seyende*] and "eternal being" [*das ewige Seyn*]. Again, they are two aspects of the same thing; in this special case, the "thing" that they both are is God or the Absolute.

Schelling uses a variety of terms to refer to the highest principle of his system, including "the Highest," the "Absolute," the "unconditioned," "absolute Indifference," "the will that wills nothing," "eternity," or "God." (These terms are not all strictly synonymous, but they can tentatively be taken to denote the same concept in different ways.) He characterizes this highest principle as inactive, resting, or indifferent, because the opposing forces of being and what-is are not in an active contradiction. It is only when this opposition is activated (by a chain of forces Schelling calls "nature" or "the eternal will") that the highest principle is drawn to resolve the contradiction, a resolution which results in the production of temporality and the revelation of God.

What-is-not (*das Nichtseyende*): Since Schelling considers being the opposite of what-is, it follows that being is not what-is; in other words, being is what-is-not. Schelling devotes much of the text to a clarification of this concept, which he insists quite firmly is distinct from "nothing" (*das Nichts*). What-is-not has a genuine ontological status, albeit a peculiar one. It is a force of negation and, as such, resists manifestation (revelation) and existence. Schelling invokes the concept of what-is-not in describing eternity's will to know itself. This will is distinct from eternity (and thus from what-eternally-is and eternal being). It is a third force, generated in eternity, and it ultimately functions to arouse what-eternally-is and eternal being into active opposition. Since its essence is longing (the longing of eternity to know itself), it is characterized by negativity and lack. This makes it an appropriate ground for a positive, outgoing essence, given the structure of grounding outlined above. A developmental sequence is formed by the initial negative force together with the positive force it grounds and the unity of the two; Schelling calls these stages *potencies (Potenzen)* and considers the overall sequence to be "nature."

Expressing/Expressed/Expressible (*das Aussprechende/das Ausgesprochene/das Aussprechliche*): Schelling uses this three-way distinction to describe the relation between the will that wills nothing and the forces dormant in eternity. The vocabulary of "expression" allows Schelling to explain his distinctive notion of identity in terms of judgment and predication.

I have translated *das Aussprechende* as "the expressing" rather than the more literal "what expresses," in order to capture Schelling's key distinction between the agent of expressing and the accomplished act of expression. Although this renders certain passages slightly more awkward, it is important that there be no ambiguity as to the fact that *das Aussprechende* is a noun.

Given the fact that Schelling's language does become somewhat cumbersome, the reader should keep in mind the following: Being and what-is are expressible of the will that wills nothing, which is their expressing. When the will that wills nothing is drawn to actually express them, they go from being merely expressible to being actually expressed. When this occurs, an aspect of the will that wills nothing, "the pure I of divinity," becomes inexpressible. There is an obvious reference, which Schelling acknowledges, to the biblical ideas of the living word and the inexpressible name of God.

In terms of man (*menschlich*): At several points in the text Schelling announces his methodological intent to interpret things "in terms of man." Although *menschlich* more literally means "humanly," I wanted to call attention to Schelling's conscious anthropomorphisms, which will undoubtedly strike the reader. Schelling considered the human to be a microcosm of forces operative on a cosmic level, and thought the individual's foundational choice of character recapitulated on a small scale God's decision to reveal himself through time.

Although the German word *Mensch* is gender-neutral, I have translated it throughout as "man." Language, as Schelling well knew, has an impetus of its own, and the term *Mensch* was associated, in the German philosophical tradition, with a masculine subject of reason, an autonomous locus of form-giving faculties. This traditional conception of the subject is clearly present in the text. At the same time, the fact that the text contains the resources to contest this traditional meaning (as Žižek points out) only adds to its rich and innovative character.

A NOTE ON THE TRANSLATION

This translation follows the German text of the 1813 draft of the *Die Weltalter* as it appears in the *Nachlassband* of Schelling's complete words, edited by Manfred Schröter (Munich: Biederstien, 1946). I have included the footnotes from Schelling's original text, as well as those of Schelling's son, Karl Friedrich A. Schelling, who edited the first collection of the philosopher's works, *F. W. J. von Schellings Sämmtliche Werke* (Stuttgart: Cotta, 1856–61). I have also kept Schöter's convention of putting into pointed brackets (the '⟨ ⟩' markings) the text that Schelling (senior) had crossed out. In addition, I used the standard Authorized Version of the English Bible to render the biblical passages (Schelling uses Martin Luther's German translation of the Bible), changing particular words when necessary to conform to the translation conventions I had adopted.

I am very grateful to Alistair Welchman and Sara Norman for their constant and devoted help, support, and advice on this project. In addition, Stephen Houlgate, Elke Henning, and other members of the philosophy department at the University of Warwick offered me good advice and friendly assistance. Whatever errors that remain are my own.

– Judith Norman

FIRST BOOK
The Past

The past is known [gewußt], the present is recognized [erkannt], the future is divined [geahndet].

What is known is recounted, what is recognized is presented, what is divined is prophesied.

Science [Wissenschaft], according to the very meaning of the word, is history [Historie] (ἱστορία). It was not able to be [history] as long as it was intended as a mere succession or development of one's own thoughts or ideas. It is a merit of our times that the essence has been returned to science; indeed, this essence has been returned in such a manner as to assure us that science will not easily be able to lose it again. From now on, science will present the development of an actual, living essence.

In the highest science what is living can be only what is primordially alive: the essence preceded by no other, which is thus the first or oldest of essences.

Since there is nothing before or outside of this primordial life by which it might be determined, it can only develop (to the extent that it does develop) freely, purely from itself alone, out of its own drive and volition. It does not, for that matter, develop lawlessly; rather, development proceeds strictly according to law. There is nothing capricious in this primordial life; it is a nature in the fullest sense of the term, just as man is a nature regardless of freedom, even because of it.

After science has attained objectivity with respect to its content, it naturally seems to follow that it would look for objectivity with respect to its form.

Philosophy has always sought to overstep the boundaries of the world – and thereby the boundaries of the present time – and to explain the first origin of things; it thus turned to the past, in the noblest sense of the term. Why was it, or has it been, impossible until now that philosophy – which is history with respect to its name and content – be history with respect to its form as well? What is known is recounted, so why can what is known of the highest science not be recounted as well, with the candidness and simplicity of everything else that is known? We can divine a golden age, a time when truth becomes fable and fable truth: but what holds this golden age back?

Man must be granted an essence outside and above the world; for how could he alone, of all creatures, retrace the long path of developments from the present back into the deepest night of the past, how could he alone rise up to the beginning of things unless there were in him an essence from the beginning of times? Drawn from the source of things and akin to it, what is eternal of the soul has a co-science/con-sciousness [Mitt-Wissenschaft] of creation.

Because this essence holds time enveloped, it serves as a link that enables man to make an immediate connection with the most ancient past as well as with the most distant future. Man often sees himself transported into such wonderful relations and inner connections through precisely this innermost essence, such as when he encounters a moment in the pressent as one long past, or a distant event as if he himself were witness to it!

Accordingly, the unfathomable, prehistoric age rests in this essence; although it faithfully protects the treasures of the holy past, this essence is in itself mute and cannot express what is enclosed within it.

Indeed, it would never open unless it were escorted by an other, itself in the process of becoming, and therefore ignorant by nature and eternally young, as the Egyptian priests said of the Greeks. Thus, to arrive at a science of things that have been, this other must turn to that inner oracle, the only witness from a time before world.

This [inner oracle], however, feels no less drawn to the other. Buried within it is the memory of all things, their original conditions, their becoming, their meaning. But this archetypal image of things slumbers within it – not, indeed, as an extinguished and forgotten image, but rather as an image growing with its own essence that it cannot take out of itself and call upon. This image would certainly never awake again, if a presentiment [Ahndung] of and longing for knowledge did not lie in that unknowing itself. But incessantly called by this [other] to its ennoblement, the higher essence notices that the lower is assigned to it, not to be held in idleness, but rather that it might have an instrument in which it could behold itself, express itself, and become intelligible to itself. For everything lies within it at the same time and without distinctions, as one; but in the other, it can distinguish and separate out what is ⟨distinguishable⟩[1] in itself.

In man, there is thus one thing that must be recalled to memory and another that recalls it; one thing in which the answer to each inquiry lies, and another thing that elicits this answer; this other is free with respect to everything and able to think anything but is bound by that first, the innermost essence, and cannot consider anything as true without the agreement of this witness. The innermost essence, in contrast, is originally bound and cannot unfold; but through the other it becomes free and opens itself out toward that other. Thus, both long for separation with equal urgency; the innermost essence so that it might move again to its original and innate knowing, and the other so that it might gain from the first essence and likewise become knowledgeable, although in an entirely different manner.

This separation, this doubling of ourselves, this secret intercourse between the two essences, one questioning and one answering, one ignorant though seeking to know and one knowledgeable without knowing its knowledge; this silent dialogue, this inner art of conversation, is the authentic secret of the philosopher from which the outer art (which for this reason is called "dialectic") is only a replica and, if it has become bare form, is only empty appearance and shadow.

Everything that is known will thus be recounted according to its nature, but what is known is not laid out as ready and accessible from the very beginning; rather, it only originates from inside by a thoroughly peculiar process. The light of science must dawn through inner separation and liberation before it can illuminate the outside. Achieved science would be history according to its form; but what we call science is only a striving to recall to con-

[1] One.

sciousness, and therefore more like an urgent quest for science than science itself. For this reason, that great man of antiquity unproblematically bestowed upon it the name "philosophy." From time to time the opinion is ventured that the most complete dialectic is to be regarded as science itself; but this reveals a restricted outlook, inasmuch as the very existence [Daseyn] and necessity of the dialectic proves that the true science (ἱστορία) has not yet been found.

Now, the philosopher finds himself in the same position as another historian. For to find what he wants to know, this latter must also question the testimony of old documents or the memory of living witnesses. He too needs considerable critical skills and discernment, to glean pure facts out of the confusion of reports and to pry apart the true from the false and the authentic from the inauthentic in the available chronicles. He too urgently requires a separation from himself, a distancing from the present, an abandonment to the past, in order to free himself of the ideas and qualities particular to his time.

Nothing whatsoever can succeed in coming immediately to consciousness, not even what is given from the outside. Everything must first become inward. If the past does not awake from within the historian himself, then he will never present it as true, as intuitive, as alive. What would all of history be, if an inner sense did not come to its aid? It would be what it is for so many who indeed know all about what has happened without understanding the slightest thing about genuine history. Not only human events but even the history of nature has its monuments, and one can well say that they do not leave a single stage along the lengthy path of creation without leaving behind a mark. These monuments of nature lie for the most part out in the open; they are thoroughly researched, in part genuinely deciphered, and yet they tell us nothing but rather remain dead until that succession of actions and productions has become inward. Thus, everything remains incomprehensible to man until it has become inward for him; that is, until it has been led back to precisely that innermost [aspect] of his essence which is for him the living witness of all truth.

Now there have always been those who thought it possible to set aside the outer instrument entirely and to abolish all duality in one's self so that we would only be inward, as it were, living entirely within the celestial realm, knowing everything immediately. Who can deny from the onset the possibility that man might ascend to his celestial principle and undergo a corresponding elevation of mental powers into an intuition [in's Schauen]? Every physical and moral whole requires for its maintenance a reduction, from time to time, to its innermost beginning. Man is rejuvenated time and again and becomes blessed anew through the feeling of unity of his nature. Those who seek science in particular continually draw fresh strength by these means; not only the poet, but the philosopher as well has his delights. He needs them in order that the feeling of indescribable reality offered by these lofty representations might protect him from the belabored concepts of a sterile and dispirited dialectic. But it is another thing to demand the persistence of an intuitional state that fights against the nature, destiny, and determination of present life. For however we may view its relation to the preceding state, the fact will always remain that what was indivisibly linked together in this state does unfold and is partially separated out. We do not live through intuitions. Our knowledge is incomplete [Stückwerk]; that is, it must be produced piecemeal [stückweis] in sections and degrees, and this cannot occur in the absence of reflection.

Accordingly, the goal is not reached through mere intuition. For there is no understanding in intuition, in and of itself. Everyone sees more or less the same things in the external world and yet cannot express it. Every thing runs through certain moments in order to attain completion: a set of processes coming one after the other where the later always intrudes on the earlier, bringing it to fruition. In plants, for example, this course can be seen by the farmer just as well as by the scholar; the farmer, however, cannot truly comprehend it because he cannot hold the moments apart, cannot separate them, cannot consider them in their mutual opposition. Likewise, a man can run through and immediately experience that sequence of processes in himself, whereby an infinite manifold is ultimately produced from the greatest simplicity of essence; indeed, to be precise, he must experience it in himself. But all experiencing, feeling, and intuiting is in and of itself mute and requires a mediating organ to gain expression. If the intuiter does not have this, or if he intentionally pushes it away from himself so that he might speak immediately from his intuition, he thereby loses the measure necessary to him: he is one with the object and, to a third [party], like the object itself. For precisely this reason, he is not master of his thoughts; he is caught in a futile struggle, expressing without any certainty what is nonetheless inexpressible; he encounters what he might, though without being sure of it, without being able to place it securely before him and, as it were, to reinspect it in the understanding as if in a mirror.

Consequently, one must on no account abandon that external principle; for all things must be brought to actual reflection so that they might achieve the highest representation. The border between theosophy and philosophy runs here, a border that the lover of science will seek to keep chaste. In terms of the depth, richness, and vivacity of content, theosophy has just as great an advantage over philosophy as does the actual object over its image, or nature over its representation; and in fact the distinction approaches incomparability when the comparison is made with a dead philosophy that looks for the essence in forms and concepts. This explains the predilection profound souls have for theosophy, which is just as easily explained as the predilection for nature in contrast to art. For theosophical systems have the advantage over all others, prevailing until now: at least they have a nature even if it is one that is not in control of itself; in contrast, the others offer nothing but un-nature and vain art. But nature is no more beyond the reach of art when properly understood than the richness and depth of life is beyond the reach of science, when properly understood; science succeeds only gradually, mediately, and through stepwise progress, so that the knower always remains distinguished from his object [Gegenstande], as it also remains separated from him and becomes the object [Object] of a calmly savored regard.

All science must pass through dialectic. But is there *never* a point at which it becomes free and alive, as when a historian, representing an image of past times, no longer thinks of his investigations? Will the memory of the primordial beginning of things never again be so vivid and alive that science may become history with respect to its outer form as well? Can the philosopher never return to the simplicity of history, as did the divine Plato, whose entire work is dialectical throughout, but becomes historical at the summit and point of transfiguration?

It seemed reserved for our age to open at least the path to this objectivity of science. To begin with, it restored the essence to science and thereby posited living development as well, whereas no living progress is possible between propositions that follow dogmatically. Furthermore, we have knowledge of the law of increase, in which alone is to be found a true beginning, a necessary and eternal base. As long as science restricted itself to the ideal, no such base was to be found. For this reason, the first steps hardly had been taken in returning life to science, when the advanced age of physicality had to be acknowledged, and how it is first with respect to all development though last with respect to dignity. Since then, science has no longer begun with thoughts drawn from far away in order to descend from these to the natural; rather, it is now the reverse: beginning with the unconscious presence [bewußtlosen Daseyn] of the Eternal, science leads it up to the supreme transfiguration in a divine consciousness. The supersensible thoughts now acquire physical force and life, while nature for its part becomes ever more the visible imprint of the highest concepts. It is, in truth, only the ignorant who still look with scorn upon the physical; but even this contempt will soon come to an end and the saying will once again prove true, that the stone the builders rejected became the cornerstone. Popularity, which is so often sought in vain, will then come on its own. There will then no longer be a difference between the world of thought and the world of reality. The world will be one, with the peace of the golden age heralded in the harmonious connection of all the sciences.

The present work will seek to defend and justify these views in a variety of ways. With such prospects, perhaps a long-pondered attempt might be hazarded, which would help make ready this future, objective presentation of science. Perhaps he will yet come, who will sing the great heroic poem, encompassing in spirit (as is reputed of the seers from times gone by) what was, what is, and what will be. But this time is not yet at hand. As its harbingers, we do not wish to pluck its fruit before it is ripe, nor do we wish to misjudge our own. This is still a time of struggle. The goal of our investigation has not yet been achieved; just as speech depends on rhythm, science depends on dialectic for accompaniment and support. We cannot recount, but only research, weighing the pros and cons of each opinion until the true one stands fast, indubitable, rooted for all time.

BOOK ONE

The Past

The past – a lofty concept, common to all and understood by only a few! Most know only of that [past] which grows within each moment through precisely that moment, and which is itself only becoming, not being. Without a present that is determined and definite, there is no [past at all]; how many have the privilege of such a past? The man who cannot separate himself from himself, who cannot break loose from everything that happens to him and actively oppose it – such a man has no past, or more likely he never emerges from it, but lives in it continually. It is advantageous and beneficial for a man to be conscious of having put something behind him, as it were – that is, of having posited it as past. The future is thereby bright and easy for him, only under the condition that there is something ahead of him. Only the man with the strength to rise above himself is able to create a true past; he alone can savor a true present, just as he alone looks forward to a genuine future; these considerations already seem to reveal that the contrast between times is founded on an increase and is not produced by time-parts flowing continuously into each other.

If, as a few supposed sages have claimed, the world were a chain of causes and effects that ran backward and forward to infinity, then there would in truth be neither past nor future. But this nonsensical thought should rightly have vanished along with the mechanistic system to which alone it belongs.

Nevertheless, if the old saying – that there is nothing new under the sun – were in some sense to prove true; and if the question "what is it that has happened?" were always correctly to be answered: "just what will one day happen"; and if the question "what is it that will happen?" were always correctly to be answered: "just that which has happened before" – then it would certainly follow that the world has in itself no past and no future. [This would entail] that everything that has happened in it from the beginning and everything that will happen up to the end belongs to a single overarching time; that the authentic past, the past as such, is what came before the world [vorweltliche]; that the authentic future, the future as such, is what will come after the world [nachweltliche]. And so a system of times would unfold for us, of which the human system would be just a copy, a repetition within a narrower sphere.

Everything that surrounds us points back to a past of incredible grandeur. The oldest formations of the earth bear such a foreign aspect that we are hardly in a position to form a concept of their time of origin or of the forces that were then at work. We find the greatest part of them collapsed in ruins, witnesses to a savage devastation. More tranquil eras followed, but they were interrupted by storms as well, and lie buried with their creations beneath those of a new era. In a series from time immemorial, each era has always obscured its predecessor, so that it hardly betrays any sign of an origin; an abundance of strata – the work of thousands of years – must be stripped away to come at last to the foundation, to the ground.

If the world that lies before us has come down through so many intervening eras to finally become our own, how will we even be able to recognize the present era without a science of the past? Even the particularities of a distinguished human individuality are often unintelligible to us before we learn about the distinctive circumstances under which the individual developed and formed. And yet we think that we can so easily discern the grounds of nature! A great work of the ancient world stands before us as an incomprehensible whole until we find traces of its manner of growth and gradual development. How much more must this be the case with such a multifariously assembled individual as the earth! What entirely different intricacies and folds must take place here! Even the smallest grain of sand must contain determinations within itself that we cannot exhaust until we have laid out the entire course of creative nature leading up to it. Everything is only the work of time, and it is only through time that each thing receives its particular character and meaning.

If, however, the true ground and beginning is also a knowledge or science of the past, or a derivation from the past, where is there a stopping point? For even when it arrives at the last visible thing, spirit still finds a presupposition that is not grounded in itself, a presupposition that indicates a time when there was nothing but the one inscrutable, self-sustaining essence, from whose depths all has come forth. Furthermore, if this is considered in the proper spirit [recht im Geiste], new abysses would be discovered in it as well. It would not be without a kind of horror that spirit would finally recognize that even in the primordial essence itself something had to be posited as a past before the present time became possible, and that it is precisely this past that is borne by the present creation, and that still remains fundamentally concealed.

I have ventured to set to writing the thoughts that have developed in me through frequently repeated consideration, thoughts concerning the organic [nature] of time and of its three great dimensions, which we distinguish as past, present, and future. I do not, however, present these thoughts in a strictly scientific form, but rather in one easy to communicate, so as to acknowledge the incompleteness of their development; for although they have long weighed on my mind, pressures of time do not allow me to give them the exposition they require.

It is easy to say – and is now a universally accepted opinion – that time is not real, that it is not independent of our mode of representation. Additionally, a false representation of the concept of time has permitted so much that is illusory and partially false to creep into the concept that it is almost pardonable to look upon it as a mere gear in our thoughts that would stop if we no longer counted days and hours. Yet everyone experiences without contradiction the essential nature of time in their own actions and affections; time can affirm its formidable reality even to those who loudly proclaim its nothingness.

It would clearly have been commendable to separate form and essence, appearance and reality, in our representations of time, if it were still the time to treat these great topics individually or in separate chapters. It is more desirable still to see everything at once in life and deed. We have a presentiment that one organism lies hidden deep in time and encompasses even the smallest of things. We are convinced (but who is not?) that each great event, each deed rich in consequence, is determined to the day, the hour – indeed to the very moment – and that it does not come to light one instant earlier than is willed by the force that stops and regulates time. Although it would certainly be much too daring to wish to gaze down into the depths of time, the moment has indeed come to develop the great system of times in its most comprehensive scope.

Whoever takes time only as it presents itself feels a conflict of two principles in it; one strives forward, driving toward development, and one holds back, inhibiting [hemmend] and striving against development. If this other principle were to provide no resistance, then there would be no time, because development would occur in an uninterrupted flash rather than successively; yet if the other principle were not constantly overcome by the first, there would be absolute rest, death, standstill and hence there would again be no time. But if we consider both of these principles to be equally active in one and the same essence, we will have contradiction straight away.

It is necessary to conceive of these principles in everything that is – indeed, in being [Seyn] itself. Every entity, everything that is, wants to be in itself and out of itself at the same time. It wants to be in itself inasmuch as it posits or collects itself together as what-is [als Seyendes], as a subject; to this extent it opposes development and expansion. It wants to be out of itself inasmuch as it desires to be what it is in itself once more, and hence externally. In the first case it is something withdrawn by itself, which sets itself in opposition to what is outside of it; but it sets itself in opposition only in order to reveal and declare itself against this outside as what it is in itself. It cannot, therefore, remain in this withdrawn condition.

Likewise with being. For considered purely as such, being is selfless and completely immersed in itself. But on precisely this account, being draws its opposite into itself and is a constant thirst for essence, a yearning to attract what-is, or to attract a subject, so that by means of this subject it might step forth from a state of mere potentiality into activity. But when being is considered as already active [wirkendes], as a being that is also again by itself, then it is necessarily already accompanied by a thing-that-is [ein Seyendes]; and this conflicts with the being, with what is based entirely in itself.

Thus, the principles we perceive in time are the authentic inner principles of all life, and contradiction is not only possible but in fact necessary.

Men seem to abhor nothing quite so much as contradiction, when it is revealed to them and compels them to action. When the contradictory nature of their situation can finally be concealed no longer, they still seek to cover it over and are blindly driven to delay the moment when action is demanded as a matter of life and death.

Just as men will want to stave off contradiction as much as possible in life, they seek an equal degree of comfort in science by decreeing as axiomatic that contradiction could never be real. But how could a law be laid down concerning something that could never in any way be real? Or, how could that axiom hold good – that is, prove itself true – when[1] contradiction was indeed nowhere to be found?

Although men – in both living and knowing – seem to shy away from nothing so much as contradiction, they still must confront it, because life itself is in contradiction. Without contradiction there would be no life, no movement, no progress; a deadly slumber of all forces. Only contradiction drives us – indeed, forces us – to action. Contradiction is in fact the venom of all life, and all vital motion is nothing but the attempt to overcome this poisoning. Therein lies the reason why, as an old book says,[2] all works that are done under the sun are full of vexation, the sun also ariseth, and the sun goeth down, only to rise up and go down again, and all things are full of labor yet do not tire, and all forces ceaselessly labor and struggle against each other.

[1] [Translator's note: reading wenn for wann]
[2] [Translator's note: this passage loosely follows Luther's translation of selections from Ecclesiastes 1.]

But since contradiction appears to be necessary, why is it so intolerable to all life such that nothing wants to persist in it but immediately strives to tear itself away? In truth, this would be unintelligible if noncontradiction were not behind all life like a permanent background, as it were, and if all living things were not attended by an immediate presentiment of this background, driving them to demand a return into it. Indeed, unless such a unity [of contradiction and noncontradiction] were acting through all things, contradiction itself would be unintelligible.

If we recognize contradiction, then we also recognize non-contradiction. If the former is motion in time, then non-contradiction is the essence of eternity. Indeed, if all of life is truly only a movement to raise itself up from contradiction, then time itself is nothing but a constant yearning for eternity. And if non-contradiction persists forever behind all contradiction, then it follows that something always persists behind and above all time that is not itself in time.

Everything longs for eternity. But how can there be something without contradiction, and hence Eternal? Is it not the case that the Highest is necessarily a thing-that-is, and yet can we deny it being? But if it is a thing-that-is, then that contradiction which we have shown to exist in everything that is will necessarily exist in it as well. The same holds true if the Highest is a being, or *has* a being, and is thus both [a being and a thing-that-is] at the same time.

And yet, as impossible as it seems to affirm both these things of the Highest, it is impossible to deny both of it as well, because it cannot possibly be what-is-not [ein Nichtseyendes], [and] cannot possibly not be.

Indeed, the Highest even seems necessarily to be both a thing-that-is and a being. For the Eternal must at the same time be the unconditioned. But what is the unconditioned? It is the essence that is from itself and comes out of itself, whose nature consists in an eternal positing-of-self or affirming. Accordingly, it can only be thought as what posits and what is posited at the same time, as what-is, and as being from itself alone. How is this contradiction to be resolved?

According to the concept of the unconditioned we have put forward, we must say that it is what-is, and yet is being as well. But this proposition itself still requires explanation.

To begin with, what is this It [Es] that is both being as well as what-is? Clearly, a twofold examination of it is possible. We can examine it to the extent that it is both what-is, as well as being; however, we must also examine it to the extent that it is merely It – in other words, simply *that which* is both being and what-is. But as *that which* is both being and what-is, it is necessarily neither the one nor the other. For as that which is both, it is the expressing [das Aussprechende] of both and can therefore be neither one of them in particular nor both at the same time; it is above both.

According to the first concept, it is thus what-is, and it is being, but it *is* not that which is both; or, to say the same thing, it is not *as* that which is both. It can only be *as* that which is both to the extent that it posits itself as the expressing of both – that is, to the extent that it actually expresses them. But if it posits itself as the expressing of both, does it actually express them? This is in no way entailed by the first concept.

The preceding is to be understood as follows. The unconditioned is what-is, and it is being. This is because it is by nature the unconditioned, without its effort, already by itself, and before it knows or posits itself as being anything.

The unconditioned is thus what-is, and it is being, although before now without its will. Moreover, there is nothing that would awaken its will actually to be both, to express itself as the one of both; for what-is differs quite distinctly from being, although the two are not outside of each other. Or, since the unconditioned is at the same time what posits and what is posited by itself, should we perhaps imagine that one part of it is what posits, and another part is what is posited? It is impossible that one part of it be exclusively what posits; for then it would, as what posits, not itself be posited. It is just as impossible that another part be exclusively what is posited; for then it would, as such, not be what posits – in other words, it would be conditioned in one part and hence would not be the absolutely unconditioned. Thus, no option remains but that it is both of these in a whole and undivided manner, and that, as what-is and as being, it is not two different essences, but rather only one essence in two different forms. If the opposites are joined together, and there is nothing able to separate them out into an active duality, then this is not the sort of opposition that sets[1] ⟨unity⟩[2] ⟨in motion,⟩ and therefore does not permit itself to be actually explained as such.

Just as the unconditioned is indeed both being and what-is, but not as *that which is* both being and what-is, likewise, the opposites are not opposites *as* such; they are, but not again *as* that which they are. They could only be opposites as such to the extent that they are expressed as such by that which is their expressing and their strength, and which alone moves them to action.

Contradiction is unthinkable without active opposition. But this is not the case at present. If what-is were actually to be posited *as* what-is, then we would immediately discern in it the conflict of those inner principles that we must recognize in everything that is. Thus, since it is what-is and yet is not posited again *as* what-is, this conflict lies buried within it. And the same holds true for being.

There are indeed those who claim to find contradiction in the very fact that one and the same thing is both what-is, and being. To this end, they call upon the so-called principle of contradiction, according to which it is impossible for one and the same thing to be both something as well as its opposite.

We wish to investigate this now, because it will help to clarify things further and is not unimportant for what follows. Properly understood, the principle of contradiction only states that the *expressing* (the essence of the copula, as one would have to say in the language of logic) can only be one.[3] However, this does not prevent ⟨the expressed⟩[4] [das Ausgesprochene] from being Two that are opposed.

Leibniz, following the Scholastics, had already remarked on the falsity of a rule that is nonetheless repeated to this day; [the

---

[1] Affects.

[2] That One and the expressing of both.

[3] Not Two, not opposed.

[4] What is connected [in the copula].

rule states that] disparate things can neither be predicated of each other nor of a third thing. For, Leibniz claimed, could one not directly counter that the soul is a body and the body a soul? They are indeed the same, for what in one respect is body is in another respect soul. One $= X$ is soul and body, which is to say one is the expressing of both, and to the extent that it actually expresses them, it is actually both as well. But to the extent that it is only their expressing – without taking into account the fact that it actually does express them – it is neither the one nor the other. The same thing holds true here. One and the same $= X$ is the expressing of both, of what-is, and of being. As such, it is neither the one nor the other; it is therefore simply one. But if it actually expresses them both then it is both, though not as the expressing but rather with respect to the expressed, just as it was both before as well, not as the expressing but indeed with respect ⟨to the expressible⟩[1] [dem Aussprechlichen].

Accordingly, there is no contradiction in the expressing as such. Would there still be contradiction in the expressible? (for we have not been speaking anywhere about the expressed). We do not wish to leave this matter uninvestigated either.

It is no doubt possible to conceive of contradiction in the expressed, but only when the contradictory elements are *equally active;* given two things that are directly opposed, if the first is posited as inactive then all contradiction would come to an end. One can say, for example, that one and the same person $= X$ is evil and is good; in other words, evil and good are expressible of one and the same person. There would indeed be a contradiction if both of these predicates were posited as active. But if one says that this person is good in terms of his actions (or as acting), then he could not be evil in the same way, namely likewise in terms of his actions. And this does not prevent us from claiming that what is not active in him – what is inert or resting – is evil; and in this way, two contradictory (contradicting, opposed) predicates can be attributed without contradiction to the same person.

In the unity – presently under consideration – of being and what-is, it is not even the case that one of these two is inactive; rather, both are inactive, for this is an inert opposition, or one in

[1] To the possibility.

which the opposites are indifferent to each other. They are present only as expressible, not even as actually expressed. For this reason, the principle of contradiction does not come into question; its application begins only when this unity comes to an end.

Since we are removing the actual opposition, the misunderstanding might set in from the other side, as if we were sublating [aufhöben] all duality, and that being and what-is were as one [einerley], not merely according to the expressing but entirely on their own. But two are always two, even when they are not posited explicitly *as* two. We can think of an eye, which in all respects is both the power of seeing and the instrument for seeing, both active and passive. Here are two things – power and instrument – that are nonetheless not *as* two, because they cannot be separated from each other or placed with each other in active opposition. Yet power and instrument are not themselves as one, but rather are eternally two. The present case is the same. We have what-is, and we have being, but the unity of the two is merely passive because the one that could express the unity does not actually express it and is itself not active. Thus, what-is and being are clearly not as two, although they are not for that matter as one; rather, they are two by nature.

There are those who understand the proposition: "One and the same thing is both what-is as well as being" in reverse, as if what-is and being were themselves one thing. Such people show themselves ignorant of the first laws of all judging. Even the careless locution "the subject is the object and the object is the subject' may not be understood in reverse. For no judgment at all, not even a proposition that is merely repeated, will affirm a oneness [Einerleyheit] of the expressed (the connected) as such. Rather, it will only affirm the oneness of what expresses (connects) them, regardless of whether this actually becomes evident as such, or is hidden, or is in fact only imagined. The true sense of each judgment – for example, that "A is B" – can only be the following: THAT *which* is = A IS THAT *which is* = B, or: THAT *which* is A and THAT *which is* B are as one. Thus, a doubling lies at the ground of even the simple concept: A in this judgment is not A, but rather is X, which is A; B is not B, but rather is X, which is B, and it is not the case that A and B are as one, either for themselves or as such:

but rather, the X which is A and the X which is B are as one. The proposition cited above ["A is B"] in fact contains three propositions: first, A is = X; second, B is = X; and only from these follows a third, A and B are the same – to wit, both are the same X.

Different conclusions can be drawn from this: for example, that the link (the "is") in the judgment is not merely a component part of the judgment, but lies at the ground of all the other parts; that the predicate and subject are both already unities for themselves, and that the link in a judgment is thus never simple, but rather is doubled with itself, as it were – a unity of unities. From this it follows further that the judgment is already preformed in the simple concept and the syllogism is already contained in the judgment; consequently, a concept is only a wrapped-up judgment and a syllogism is an unfolded judgment. I set these remarks to writing with an eye toward a highly desirable future treatment of the noble art of reason. For although knowledge of the universal laws of judging by no means constitutes the highest science itself, it is indeed so essentially interconnected with the highest science that they cannot be separated. But we do not philosophize for beginners or those ignorant of the art of reason; such people should rather be sent back to school, as happens in other arts, since nobody will venture lightly to put forward or judge a musical work without having learned the first laws of composition.

It is clearly impossible for what-is, as such, ever to be being, as such, and vice versa; it is also impossible for *opposites* as such to be one. We do not need to insist on these points, since to claim the opposite would be to do away with common sense, with the possibility of expressing oneself, and indeed, with the contradiction itself. Yet it is surely possible that *one and the same* thing be both what-is and being, affirming and negating, light and darkness, good and evil.

We could not avoid this dialectical discussion. It is essential that this first idea be brought into sharp focus, that no more and no less be thought in it than it contains.

No more; which would be the case if one were to think of [the unity of being and what-is] as an actually expressed unity. If one were to say that an unexpressed opposition is inactive and hence dead – then that is just what it would be. For the essential thing in scientific progression is to recognize the boundary of each moment and to focus on it sharply; [we must take care] not to anticipate, not to be rash, as this would spoil the project from the outset, as happens with most of those who engage in such an undertaking.

No less; which would happen if one wished to think all duality as sublated, because one and the same thing is both what-is and being.

The discussion to this point has only prepared us to resolve this initial contradiction. By way of a summary, we could explain ourselves thus: According to the first idea, the Eternal is *what-is,* and is *being;* or, both of these are expressible of the Eternal, although they are indeed not expressed. But it itself, which is *them,* or of which they are expressible, can as such be neither the one nor the other, but only the expressing of both. That the Eternal actually expresses them and reveals itself as expressing them both – this is not posited with the first idea.

The opposition (of what-is and being) is thus present; but what could express it does not actually express it. The expressing is present as well, but it does not attend to the opposition; it is indifferent toward it. This indifference [Gleichgültigkeit] that we have also considered elsewhere under the name of absolute *Indifferenz* [absolute Indifferenz] of subject and object, we call the absolutely First [das schlechthin Erste].

We can therefore say of *this* – which is supposed to express the opposition but does not – that it both *is* what-is as well as being, and yet *is not* [what-is and being].

It *is* what-is and it *is* being, because there is a thing-that-is and there is being, and it could express these; or: it is what-is and it is being, with respect to the expressible, to the possible. It is not what-is, nor is it being with respect to itself or in deed, because it does not attend to the opposition. But if something does not attend to what it is, it is not actual.

It can therefore be said without contradiction that the unconditioned is not what-is and it is not being, and yet it is not what-is-not, and it is not nonbeing.

The unconditioned can express itself as what-is and as being, and it can refrain from expressing itself as both; in other words, it can be both, or it can let both alone. Free will is just this ability to be something along with the ability to not-be it.

But further, the Highest can be what-is, and it can be being; it can express itself as this thing-that-is, and as this being. That is, it can express itself or posit itself as *existing*. For existence [Existenz] is precisely the active unification of a definite thing-that-is with a definite being.

Put most succinctly: the Highest can exist, and it can also not-exist; this is to say it has all conditions of existence in itself, but what matters is whether or not it draws upon these conditions, whether it uses them as conditions.

A thing that is free, not either to be *something* or not to be it, but rather to exist or not to exist – such a thing, by itself and with respect to its essence, can only be *will*. For only pure will is free to become active (that is, to exist) or to remain inactive (that is, not to exist). It alone is allowed to stand in the middle as it were, between being and nonbeing. Thus, that expressing which is free (with respect to its essence) to attend to or not to attend to opposition, to affirm or not to affirm itself as what-is and as being – this can only be pure, unmitigated will.

But to the extent that it refrains from opposition and does not actually express itself as what-is and as being – to that extent, it is not absolute will. But it certainly is will to the extent that it does not *actually* will, or is the tranquil will.

Thus, we will now say that the unconditioned, the expressing of all essence, of everything that is and of all being – considered exclusively in itself – is pure will in general. But this same thing, with respect to its indifference toward what-is and toward being (or, to say the same thing, toward existence), this is precisely that [state of] noncontradiction for which we have been looking; it is the *will that wills nothing*.

It is thus not the case, as is often said (as befits the restless essence of the time), that a deed, an unconditioned activity or action is the First. For the absolutely First can only be that which the absolutely Last can be as well. Only an immovable, divine – indeed, we would do better to say supradivine – indifference is absolutely First; it is the beginning that is also at the same time the end.

If activity in general, or a particular deed or action were the First, then contradiction would be eternal. But movement never occurs for its own sake; all movement is only for the sake of rest. If all acting did not have the calm and restful will in the background, it would annihilate itself; for all movement seeks only rest, and rest is its nourishment or that from which alone it takes its power and sustains itself.

But if the will that wills nothing is the expressing of eternity, then it is not true that it has nothing that it *could* will; on the contrary, it has what is eternally willed of itself (itself alone, as subject and object, as the authentic essence), but it has it *as if it did not have it* and is for this reason alone the *resting, the indifferent* will. To be as if one were not, to have as if one had not; that is in man, that is in God, the Highest of all.

To the common man who has never felt true freedom, the Highest always seems to be a thing-that-is or a subject. Thus, when he hears that what expresses the divine is neither a thing-that-is nor being, he asks: what could be thought above all being and everything that is? To this he answers: nothing, or something similar.

It is indeed nothing, but in the same way that pure freedom is nothing. It is nothing in the same way as the will that wills nothing, that desires no object, to which all things are equal, and which is therefore moved by none. Such a will is nothing, and yet it is everything. It is nothing to the extent that it neither desires to become active nor craves any actuality. It is everything, because all strength comes from it alone as the eternal freedom; because it has all things under it, and because it rules all things and is ruled by none.

Negation generally means very different things, depending on whether it is referred to the inside or the outside. For the highest negation in the last [i.e., outer] sense must be one with the highest affirmation in the first [inner sense]. What ⟨has⟩[1] everything in itself can for precisely that reason ⟨not⟩[2] have it ⟨at the same time⟩ externally. Everything has qualities through which it is recognized and grasped; and the more qualities it has, the more

[1] Is.
[2] Nothing.

graspable it is. That which is superlative is complete and without qualities. Taste – that is, the talent for making distinctions – finds nothing to taste in the sublime, as little as in water drawn from the source. One of the ancients has said that he is king who hopes for nothing and fears nothing. So too, in a play by an old German author – rich in meaning, full of intensity – the will is called poor that,[1] because it has everything in itself, has nothing outside itself that it can will or want.

This is the sense in which we wish to call this pure freedom by itself the nothing, if this is taken to mean that no externalizing qualities or effects are ascribed to it. We will go still further: when the name *something* is reserved for what is externally present – at least for itself – or what posits itself, then we cannot allow this highest purity to be considered "something" in the same sense. It is the pure freedom itself that does not grasp itself, it is the composure [Gelassenheit] that thinks about nothing and rejoices in its nonbeing.

There is a question that gets raised in childhood but grows tiring in mature age: "where has everything come from?" But where everything has come from can be nowhere else than where everything is still coming from and where everything is going back to, and which was thus not only *before* time but is still in every moment constantly *above* time.

For these reasons as well, the immovable will that wills nothing is First and Highest. For the will that wills nothing always penetrates through the greatest turmoils of life and the most violent movement of all forces. Everything aims for it, everything longs for it. Every created thing, every man in particular strives, in truth, only to return to the condition of nonwilling; not only he who strips himself away from all desirable things, but – though unknowingly – also he who abandons himself to all desires. For this man too desires only the state in which he has nothing more to wish for, nothing more to want, even if that state retreats immediately from him; and the more zealously he pursues, the further away it is.

---

[1] ⟨because it relies on nothing⟩ because it is itself sufficient, has nothing that it can will or want.

And just as the will that wills nothing is Highest in man, so too in God himself – this very will is above God. For under God we can only think of the highest good, which is an already determined will. But in the will that wills nothing there is neither this nor that, neither good nor evil, neither what-is nor being, neither affection nor aversion, neither love nor wrath, and yet the strength to be all of them.

We thus recognize the will that wills nothing as the expressing, the I of the eternal, unbeginning divinity itself, which can say of itself: I am the alpha and the omega, the beginning and the end.

So before we enter onto the long dark way of the [various] times, we must endeavor to recognize that which in all time is above time.

Now the great riddle of all times originates precisely here, the riddle of how anything could have come from what is neither externally active nor is anything in itself. And yet life did not remain in that state of immobility, and time is just as certain as eternity. Indeed, to the casual glance the latter even seems driven out by the former; a world full of movement, full of conflict and strain of all forces seems to have taken over the place where the highest indifference, eternal rest, and universal satiation once dwelt.

There have always been those who claimed that this riddle was easy to solve. The unconditioned, they say, is at first purely in itself, devoid of externalization and hidden; but now it steps out, externalizes itself, and sublates its eternal indifference by itself. But these are words without sense. It is a founding and principle rule of science (though few know it) that what is posited once is posited forever and cannot be sublated again, since otherwise it might just as well not have been posited at all. If one does not remain steadfastly by what one has once posited, then everything will become fluid as it progresses, and everything will wear away again, so that in the end nothing really was posited. True progress, which is equivalent to an elevation, takes place only when something is posited permanently and immutably and becomes the ground of elevation and progression. Thus, either the Highest is not a restful will (such as we have assumed) or it is one. If it is one, then it must also eternally remain as such from itself. For it is entirely incomprehensible how the Highest could cross over from rest into motion. Thus it can neither emerge from itself, nor can it separate off or emit something from itself, nor can it produce anything outside of itself.

It is by no means easy to express what is true correctly and appropriately. Yet we will do best here to take everything in terms of man and as naturally as possible. For the course that we shall undertake to describe can indeed be none other than that through which nature, at first resting and unconscious of itself, comes in and to itself alone.

We understand eternity to mean the whole: what-eternally-is [das ewige Seyende] and being, as well as the (still-concealed) expressing of both; as such, eternity is not conscious of itself. The opposites therefore cannot separate from each other, and for this reason cannot approach each other either. What-is does not oppose itself to being and does not recognize itself in being. Being is, for its part, perfectly indifferent toward what-is. But the more this composure is profoundly deep and intrinsically full of bliss, the sooner must a quiet longing produce itself in eternity, without eternity either helping or knowing. This is a longing to come to itself, to find and savor itself; it is an urge to become conscious *of which Eternity itself does not become conscious.* We can imagine the separated poles of a magnet to be in a state of constant, unconscious longing, by virtue of which they strive to come to each other and would eagerly seize hold of any means available to reach each other. Similarly, we may imagine the eternal opposition [of being and what-is] to be a state of mutual, unconscious longing and yearning for each other, although they do not know each other. This longing, however, does not become action or motion. The only perfect similarity would be with human nature in its first becoming and progress toward active existence. But who is able to describe the first stirrings of a nature that lacks consciousness, a nature that does not know itself? Who can unveil the secret birthplace of existence? Think! – have you ever enjoyed those rare moments of such blissful and perfect fulfillment, when the heart desires nothing, when you could wish these moments to remain eternally as they are, and when they actually are like an eternity to you? Think of this and try to remember how, in just such moments, a will is already at work producing itself, although unbeknownst to you and without your effort – indeed, you could not prevent this production. This will soon pulls you back to yourself; it tears you away, back into the activities of life. Remember this, and you will have an approximate picture of what we are presently undertaking to describe.

Everything that is something without actually being it must by nature seek itself; but this is not to say that it will find itself, and still less that a movement or a going out from itself takes place. This is a seeking that remains silent and completely unconscious, in which the essence remains alone within itself, and is all the more profound, deep, and unconscious, the greater the fullness it contains in itself. If we could say that the resting will is the First, then we can also say that an unconscious, tranquil, self-seeking will is the Second.

Since eternity is unconsciously impelled to seek itself, a self-sufficient will *produces* itself in eternity. *Eternity is not conscious of this will,* [whose production occurs] independently of it, and in a manner unintelligible to it. The will, for its part, does not yet know eternity but has only a presentiment of it; it seeks the essence blindly and without the assistance of eternity, not as a conscious will but rather as a will that is initially unconscious.

This will *produces itself* and is therefore unconditioned and *in itself* omnipotent; it produces itself absolutely – that is, out of itself and from itself. Unconscious longing is its mother, but she only conceived it and it has *produced* itself. It produces itself not *out* of eternity, but rather *in* eternity (which is no different from how a will unconsciously produces itself in a man's mind without his effort, a will that he does not make but only *finds,* and that only when found becomes a means for him to externalize what lies innermost within him). Thus, because it does not produce itself *out* of eternity but rather *in* it, it is itself an *eternal will* – indeed it is to be considered the *eternal will* per se, since the will that wills nothing was only the pure willing of eternity by itself. (And, according to an old rule, that which does not exist actively can have no predicates ascribed to it.) We simply cannot think about this in terms of becoming or beginning out of some preceding state of affairs, since before the will produced itself eternity

137

was as nothing and hence could not actively precede anything else nor be the beginning of anything. Eternity *was,* but it was what your "I" was before it found itself and felt itself; it was, but as if it were not. All beginning that itself begins exists only by [virtue of] the active will, which in this manner is its own beginning, as we will show.

The will produces itself in eternity *without* eternity knowing and remains, with respect to its ground, concealed from eternity. But eternity is concealed from the will as well, and since the will produces itself in the unconscious state of longing, it does not really know what it does or whether it is not simply blind; for the will seeks eternity, driven not by knowledge but rather by divination, presentiment, and inexpressible longing.

For just these reasons, although the will is independent of eternity (and in a sense even opposed to it), it does not sublate eternity as many would like to imagine. For this is the very will that wills eternity – that wills that the will that wills nothing become active and perceptible to itself *as such.* Eternity must therefore endure, because the will seeks it and could not otherwise find it. Furthermore, because the will seeks eternity, it can – for precisely this reason – never become *eternity itself;* rather, it is eternally only a will that wills and desires eternity.

But it is indeed only the *will* toward eternity, and it is not the case that the will has actually found it yet. There is thus something negated in this will; but beginning lies in negation alone. There is no beginning in that which is everything, and for this reason there can be no beginning in eternity.

The eternal will alone provides the initial point that starts up the great process of the whole. It posits itself as the mere *willing* of eternity, and to that extent as negated. But in positing itself as negated, it is at the same time the self-negating will. Yet it cannot negate itself by positing itself as not being at all; rather, it can only posit itself as not being the *essence,* or what affirms, or what-(genuinely and by nature)-*is.* Moreover, the will cannot negate itself as being the essence without positing itself as lack [Mangel] and – to the extent that it is also active – as hunger, as yearning, as desire for essence. Returning into itself, it necessarily finds itself to be empty and in need but is for that reason all the more eager to fill itself, to satiate itself with essence. But it finds essence neither inside itself nor outside itself; for it does not recognize eternity, and by returning into itself it is turned much more away from eternity than toward it. Thus, nothing is left but for the will to posit essence or affirmation absolutely outside of itself through an unconditioned and totally generative force.

The will *generates* essence in the authentic sense of the term, because essence was not essence as such before the will, and because the will does not posit essence *within* itself but rather *outside* of itself, as an essence distinct from it, free of it, indeed foreign and opposed to its nature. Since the will recognizes itself as not being what-is, and to that extent as *what-is-not,* it recognizes, by contrast, the essence, what affirms, as what-(authentically and in-itself)-*is.*

Now nature presents itself simply as a will whose character is to be negated and to negate itself, but which becomes in this negation an eternal desiring and positing of essence and of what-truly-is; even considered as a generative force, the primary negating willing cannot be expressed in any other way. Everyone will recall the opinion typical of the ancients, according to which nature (or, as they also say, matter) is fundamentally poverty, lack of essence, and the greatest need; but that it is also constantly greedy for form, for spirit, for essence and for what-genuinely-is. Genuine essence, which poverty strives to wed, is presented by contrast as richness and excess itself, as effusively and inexhaustibly communicative.

If we regard nature in its initial stages, we find an attracting, inward-returning force in all corporeal things; this force never appears for itself alone, but only ever as the bearer of another essence, fastening it down and holding it together. This other essence is expansive by nature, and it is thus volitilizing and spiritualizing. If there were no negating force, then this other essence would have nothing against which it could externalize itself and through which it could be put into effect. But without this overflowing and communicative essence, the attracting force would be empty and genuinely ineffectual, unfulfilled and unbearable [unleidlich] to itself. Where nature opens itself up to our instruments of sensation, we feel this very negating and contracting force as coldness; but this force is only *sharp* or actual and sensible cold to the extent that it pulls itself in and hungers for that freely effluent, charitably communicative, all-liberating essence of heat. If there were no cold, then heat would not be perceptible, for without a force that holds together and restricts, heat would lose itself in its infinite expansion. If there were no heat, then cold would be senseless as well, since it only exists in order for heat to be generated and become perceptible. And thus we see nature – from the lowest level upward, in its very innermost principles and most profound concealment, voraciously rising up and striding forth in its quest until it has finally taken the highest essentiality, the purely spiritual itself, has drawn it into itself and made it its own.

Accordingly, we recognize that this will, generated out of itself in the tranquillity of eternity, was the eternal will to nature, if we understand by this not the merely negated and self-negating principle, but rather the revealed essence that became external through this principle. For only with nature does opposition, distinction, and the mutual externality and perceptibility of forces begin.

But all of this – the entire fullness and future splendor of nature – is only built upon the ground of an eternal, self-negating will that returns into itself, and without which nothing could be revealed anywhere.

People are generally opposed to what negates and demonstrate a natural preference for what affirms. They understand what-is, since it is communicative and freely gives of itself; but they frankly cannot comprehend what denies and negates itself – even if it is just as essential and is encountered everywhere in many forms. Most people, being as they are, would find nothing so simple as a world made of pure love and goodness, even though they must soon become aware of the opposite. A counterstriving imposes itself everywhere; everyone feels this other force, which, as it were, should not be, but nevertheless is – indeed, it must be. [It is] this No that opposes the Yes, this darkness that opposes the light, this crooked that opposes the straight, this left that opposes the right, or however else people have always sought to exhibit this eternal opposition in images. But one is not easily in a position to express this opposition, or to comprehend it at all scientifically.

In particular, the concept of what-is-not has always been a true Proteus, leading to much confusion and many errors.

We hardly need to be reminded that the concept [of what-is-not] as it is presented here must not be confused with the earlier concept, from which the claim emerged: the Highest cannot be expressed as a thing-that-is. For the Highest was not *a thing-that-is*, because it is above what-is; the ancients too had already expressed it as such, (as a ὕπερον). What-is-not, which is the topic at hand, is, on the contrary, *under* what-is.

But very few people have realized that true force lies in limitation and not in expansion, and that more strength belongs to self-denial than to self-indulgence. It is thus also natural that when most people come across any form of what-*(through itself)*-is-not, they see it as a robbery of all essence, as a complete nothing. Accordingly, they claim that it can in no way be and denounce as the greatest of contradictions any teaching that claims that it exists precisely *as* what-is-not.

We will not dwell on the opinions of such people, for these have already been dispelled through our derivation of what-is-not. We have shown that it posits *itself* as what-is-not. But precisely in denying that it is what-is, it necessarily shows its greatest force; indeed, we would do better to say that it thereby proves to be force and strength itself. It is well known that the divine Plato already taught, with the greatest generality, how necessary what-is-not really is, and how without this insight certainty would remain everywhere indistinguishable from doubt as would truth from error. Given the manner in which we have been speaking, we could now present the point as follows: the negating force is *being* to the true essence or to what-is. Being, according to the very concept, cannot be as one with what-is; instead (as its opposite), being is by nature *what-is-not*, although it is for that matter certainly not the nothing (as in the false translation of the Greek οὐκ ὄν, from which the concept of the creation from nothing seems to have originated as well). For how could that which is being and the force of being itself, be the nothing? Being, after all, must be itself. There is no mere being, nothing that is purely, vacuously objective in which there is nothing subjective. What-is-not is specifically what-*subjectively*-is-not; yet it is in fact what-*nonsubjectively*-is. It is only what-is-not in contrast to what-subjectively-is, since this latter has priority in terms of what-is; but solely with reference to itself, it is likewise what-is. To it, what-is-not is only its external aspect, revealed to the other; what-is is only its internal aspect and concealed. Put the other way around, we can meanwhile infer from the opposition that being or the negative is only latent in what-is, while what-is, or the positive principle, is revealed and active. An inner, qualitative unity of both would appear at the same time, which we only indicate here because it might prove important for what follows.

But another sort of sophistry misuses the concept of what-is-not in another way. For this concept is supposed to serve as a proof that being is not comprehensible [erkennbar], from which this sophistry further concludes that absolutely nothing is comprehensible. For it does not know how to raise itself above blind feeling, which actually has only an immediate reference to being. Because being is based on darkness with respect to its force, or on an active opposition to essence and everything related to essence, it seems inexpressible and incomprehensible; or, as one of the ancients has said in a different context, only comprehensible to the noncomprehending. Consequently, this sophistry drew the conclusion that all knowing that actually knows dissolves and destroys being, and that true knowing could only consist in non-knowing. An incomparable doctrine – to serve the interests of comfort! For the Real is, precisely on account of [its problematic relation to comprehension], all the less easy to comprehend and harder to penetrate. It requires diligence and mental effort to become comprehensible; in contrast, the Ideal is more easily and immediately comprehended, because it is by nature related to what comprehends. But as to the conclusion that these sophists draw from the concept of what-is-not against the possibility of knowledge, this is how things stand.

It is certainly the case that only what-is is intrinsically comprehensible, while what-is-not is not comprehensible. But what-is-not is ungraspable only insofar as and to the extent *that* it is not; to the extent that, as what-is-not, it nonetheless *is*, to that extent it is indeed graspable and comprehensible. What-is-not and what-is are not two different essences in it but are rather only one essence regarded from different sides. That by virtue of which it is not, is the very thing by virtue of which it is. For it is not due to a lack of light and essence that it is not, but rather as a dynamic hiding-away, an active striving backward into the depths, into concealment, and therefore as an active force that likewise *is* – and hence is comprehensible.

So much then, toward a dialectical engagement with the concepts of what-is and what-is-not, which are of the greatest importance for the entire consequence of the science.

The will that produces itself through itself without the knowledge of eternity – this will is the first distant beginning toward a revelation [Offenbarung]. Without deliberation, driven by dark presentiment and longing, it posits itself as negated, as not being what-is. But it negates itself only in order to reach essence. In negating, it is thus immediately an eternal seeking and desiring of essence; and precisely in so desiring, it posits essence as in itself independent of it, as the eternal good itself, as that which alone deserves to have being in itself.

Yet through this negating, the negating will finds itself in opposition to the freely outpouring essence; it finds itself to be strictness and severity as opposed to the mildness of the essence, to be darkness as opposed to the light, to be an eternal No that conflicts with the Yes.

But the will seeks indifference[1] – or rather it longs for indifference with a presentiment that is not knowledge. Thus, through a progressive effect of its desiring force, the will posits for itself indifference, or the unity that liberates it from conflict and allows it to recognize itself as one with its opposite. But this unity is spirit, although[2] spirit at a lower level; for spirit is that in which being and what-is (for this is how we have shown the negating will and the affirming essence – which is also a will – to act), two opposed wills, Yes and No, distinguish themselves from each other and recognize themselves as belonging to a single essence.

[1] Eternity.
[2] Because it climbs up from under.

143

With the generation of spirit, the goal is necessarily attained, for there is nothing higher to produce. Thus, the totality of principles operates through a progressive generation of the first desiring will. For all principles are invoked in the negating, inward-returning force, in the affirming, self-expanding essence and in the active, free, living unity of both, which is spirit. Generating cannot take place over and above spirit; spirit is that in which generation reposes, in which generation grasps itself and attains eternity, and for that reason comes to a standstill.

This progressive generation can be represented as an increase. If one posits the affirming principle as such = A and the negating principle as such = B, then the first active will is indeed in itself what-is, but it also negates itself as such. It is thus an A that acts as such = B; that is = (A = B). This is the beginning, and hence the first potency [Potenz]. But this A posits itself by itself as negated only in order to posit the true essence as free, active, and independent of it; now to the extent that this acts as what-is of a thing-that-is [das Seyende eines Seyenden] = (A = B), it can be considered as what-is of the second potency = A^2. Finally, unity or spirit, as the common affirming of both A and B, can be seen only as what affirms the third potency = A^3. Thus, all generation is completed in three potencies, and through three stages the productive force achieves spirit.

If we observe all of the principles in their relation, it is clear that the ground of their actualization, distinguishability and mutual externality lies in the initial will alone. If the eternal will – that original force of negating – could ever stop working, everything would return into nothing and it would again be nothing[1] as it once had been. But after this force achieves totality and recognizes itself in the unity of spirit, this one-sided relation cancels itself again [hebt sich auf]. For the affirming essence eternally calls for the negating will, in order that it might eternally be generated from this will and rise up over it as the essence. On the other hand, the attracting force eternally calls for the freely effluent, affirming will, in order that it might fulfill its desire for essence through this affirming will. Furthermore, unity or spirit eternally calls for the opposites, because it can be generated only

[1] The ineffectual eternity.

through progressive increase by means of this opposition. But opposition, for its part, also eternally calls for unity or spirit, because only in spirit can it become conscious of itself, grasp itself, and comprehend itself as eternity. Here then is the highest inner harmony, the most freely willed concord and euphony of the principles. They are all mutually external and free from each other, each one is its own principle which has its own root in itself; and yet they are coherently joined, not through an external link, but rather are connected to each other through an inner necessity. Just such a free belonging-together, with an exclusively inner, not outer inseparability, can be characterized with the precise scientific term: *totality*.

This is not the tranquil unity that subsists in eternity, a quiet unity that is imperceptible to itself; here we find actual opposition, ⟨but⟩[1] not one that is sparked into conflict. The forces interact with each other, but they act only to the extent that they are forces – that is, to the extent that they are active by nature and not posited by an external cause to be in tension with each other. The forces become perceptible to each other, but without fighting each other. This is the first pure joy of mutual finding and being found. Essence should, by right, be *in-itself,* and it is not without bliss that it senses its first and purest reality; the negating power, for its part, rejoices in the soothing of its harshness and severity, in the quieted hunger of its attracting desire. For unity or for spirit, however, the opposition serves as an eternal pleasure [Lust], since spirit only becomes sensible to itself in the opposition; and far from sublating this opposition, spirit seeks instead to constantly posit and confirm it. But those opposites rejoice just as much in the discovered unity, in which they have also become conscious and have been delivered from blind essence; they hold fast to this unity with all forces. Now because the opposites are not bound to each other or to unity by a necessary link, but rather only by the inexhaustible pleasure of having and feeling the presence of each other, this is the freest life, the life that plays with itself, as it were, filled with ceaseless excitement and bursting with its own renewed vitality.

[1] Although.

Moreover, if we wish to engage in a dialectical consideration of the unity achieved by these principles, there is an opportunity to do so, since there is no contradiction in the fact that the opposites are equally active and yet posited as one. The contradiction is solved as follows. The opposites are one, which is to say that a unity of both is posited; here $= A^3$. But in spite of this, they are supposed to be actively opposed, or equally active as opposed. Since they cannot be opposed to the extent that they are in unity, they must at the same time be out of unity – that is, separated and each for itself. In other words, there is opposition as well as unity; opposition is free with respect to [gegen] unity, and unity with respect to opposition; or unity and opposition are themselves in opposition. There is nothing contradictory here, for opposition in and of itself is not a contradiction. But if the unity of unity and opposition were posited, then contradiction would incontestably be found.

Now this would be the most excellent and perfect unity, since the conflicting elements are free and yet at the same time one, and free movement neither cancels unity nor does unity cancel free movement. Even when this type of unity presents itself on perhaps a lower level, it still deserves to be kept in mind and indeed comprehended. If we wanted to find something similar, the most fitting comparison would probably be with the unity of forces of which one becomes aware in the innocence of youth. There, all forces are indeed present and in natural interaction amongst themselves, excited by gentle interplay; but no character, no I-hood, no one has yet stepped forth to dominate and control them. It is often said that this condition of innocence serves as a pattern for one which we will attain again, through the highest strife of all forces, after eventual reconciliation. Similarly, it is not impossible that this sort of unity (which appears to us here as still on a lower level) would be the pattern for a future unity that life is to win back after constant struggle, in the highest transfiguration.

Now is the time to pose the following question: in what relation does this entire life that has arisen from below stand to eternity or to that unmoving indifference? For life can be given its complete determination only in reference to eternity.

This entire life, after all, originated in the first place out of the longing of eternity for itself. In searching for itself and yet not being able to find itself, the will produced itself in an urgent manner, desiring eternity and seeking contact with it. Through progressive increase, this will has now constructed a series of steps by which it can ascend to eternity. For spirit – or the highest unity produced through its desire – is by nature one with indifference or eternity. For this reason, spirit is not only the unity of the opposites, as was assumed until now; it is at the same time the link between eternity and the life built up from below, a life that already presents itself ever more clearly as the instrument of eternity.

If the productive force is nothing other than the force or first will to nature, then the totality it generates is even now the external, visible (if not yet seen) aspect of a God who is still concealed in eternity and who will (according to revelation) appear in the future. But through progressive increase, as it approaches that free unity which we can already express as consciousness and spirit, the essence of the once blind will is no longer merely presentiment, but now feels and knows the present divinity. Achieving the goal of its longing, this will pulls eternity to itself and calls upon eternity to recognize this external being (which is still, as we have shown, self-less) and posit it as eternity's own being.

The spirit that has arisen from below comes specifically from what is objective. For this reason, it has an immediate relation only to what is objective[1] of eternity [zu dem Objectiven der Ewigkeit], and not to what-is, which rests in eternity. Only what is the object in eternity is *essentially* equal to the subject and relates to the external or the visible itself as the purest spirit – and accordingly as subject.

Because nature desires this eternal spirit and pulls what is objective of eternity to itself as its immediate subject, it first makes a division in eternity. As a result, eternal being actually becomes an object to what-eternally-is, although nature does not thereby sublate the indifference. For eternity is in itself (or apart from the attraction of nature) still the same indifference of subject and object, and it must always remain so, since otherwise nature itself would retreat.

[1] To the being.

147

Since nature therefore pulls that purest spirit – what is objective of eternity – to itself, all forces assume passive qualities in comparison with spirit as their higher, authentic subject, and they sink down, becoming material for it. The first, most tender, corporeality arises; the affirming, freely effluent principle, bound by its opposite, becomes a tempered thing of light – but the harsh or negating force is soothed and transfigured through the light and the mildness of the other. Yet it is only facing above that the active forces, which have been spiritual until now, assume corporeal qualities as well; considered in themselves or facing downward, and in comparison with the now corporeal matter, they are pure spirit and life.

This first corporeal state itself has a corporeal and a spiritual side. For the body proper is the opposition in which spirit immediately clothes itself, as with a transparent wrapping. The unity, however, is spirit. Spirit is passive toward what is above, in order to pull the above to itself; but it is active and effective toward what is below, with the force taken from above. The whole is thus a spiritual-corporeal essence, and even at this early stage, the spiritual and the corporeal find themselves to be the two sides of one and the same existence.

There have always been many who fervently desired to penetrate this tranquil realm of the past and thereby genuinely get to the bottom of the great process in which they are partly spectators and partly coacting and compassionate [mitleidende] participants. But most people lack the requisite humility; they wish to begin[1] everything straight away with the highest concepts and bypass the mute beginnings of all life. And if something is now barring the reader's way into this world before time, it is just this overhasty nature that would rather bedazzle from the very start with spiritual concepts and clichés than descend to the natural beginnings of every life.

Although we are positing the unbeginning eternal divinity above all being, we make no secret of our claim that nature's priority with respect to revealed, active existence is just as certain. As high as we place actuosity [Actuosität] in any other respect,

[1] [*Marginal addition by Schelling's son:* seize hold of.]

we must indeed deny that it is the First.[1] For even that essence in which the active will first produced itself has more of a passive than an active manner (if these concepts are at all applicable here). A merely germinal (potential) life precedes the active. I find it plausible for many reasons that in organic nature the receptive sex is present first and on its own, and that the supposedly asexual character of the lower species of animals is based partly on this.

But perhaps some will try to dispute the priority [of nature over active existence] in the present case using accepted universal conceptions such as, for example, the familiar idea that God is of himself the essence with the most actuosity. Granted, this is said easily enough and certainly excuses us from all further investigations. However, this concept is not one that is necessarily found, but is rather an arbitrary, unexamined assertion, a truly a priori concept in the bad sense of that term. But other responses are less meaningful still; for example, some will object that in this manner, physicality gets mixed in with God. Yet in the sense that this could be true, the claim that God is the Master and Creator of nature does not avoid this admixture either. In addition, people have appealed long enough to the idea that God is the ground of his own existence. Is this notion of "ground" just an empty word, or does it denote something real? If it is just a word, then let us be more accurate and not allow ourselves to use senseless words. [On the other hand, if the ground is something real,] then people must themselves acknowledge that there was something before the existing God *as such* that did not itself exist because it was only the ground of existence. Now, that which is only the ground of existence cannot have an essence and qualities that are as one with what exists; and if existence is to be regarded as free, conscious, and (in the highest sense) intelligent, then what is merely the ground of its existence cannot be conscious, free, and intelligent in the same sense. Moreover, since most people call the opposite of these qualities "physical," let them now see whether they themselves have not unknowingly attributed a primacy of the physical in God, despite their repugnance at the thought.

[1] With respect to revelation.

If such people refuse to recognize anything at all natural or physical in God, then they must not acknowledge anything outside of absolute purity or indifference. For only this, the purest divinity, is natureless, because it is the eternal freedom itself and above all being. But these people crudely declare precisely this divinity or freedom to be nothing, and understand by this term what is truly to be called nothing. Where then is their God?[1]

And besides, what is it that leads most people to slander matter as they do? In the end, it is only the modesty of matter that is so offensive to them. But this very composure proves that something dwells within matter, something of that original essence, of the germ and primordial material of existence, something that is passive on the outside but is in itself the purest spirituality.

It is easy to see that the main difficulty with the current way of philosophizing lies in its lack of intermediary concepts. For instance, what is not morally free is straightaway mechanistic, what is not spiritual in the highest sense is corporeal, and what is not intelligent is wholly without reason. But intermediary concepts are precisely the most important; indeed, they are the only genuinely explanatory concepts in the whole of science. Someone who wishes to think only according to the so-called principle of contradiction may be clever at disputing the pros and cons of everything, just like the sophists, but will be fully incapable of discovering truth, which does not lie at the far-flung extremes.

Thus, the idea of matter that is in or of itself spiritual and incorporeal will appear completely unfathomable to many people. We wish to remind such people how [this supposedly unfathomable idea] fundamentally already involves the well-known theory of the construction of matter out of forces, which states that the inner essence of all matter is spiritual in a broad sense, since forces are undeniably something incorporeal, and to that extent spiritual. At the same time, this remark proves that the nature of present corporeal matter is not (as is claimed) explicable by those inner, spiritual forces in and of themselves. To the extent that the inner or pure essence of matter is produced by these forces alone, it must itself be spiritual. And if corporeality is not an internally founded state, then it must be the result of an external force that

[1] [*Translator's note*: Psalms 42:3.]

is separate from matter and worked on it as a contracting, coagulating potency.

For these reasons, anyone who attempts a merely dynamic construction of matter must be led to conclude that its original condition was spiritual. If this is the case, we can go further and claim what necessarily follows, that this spiritual matter is still to this day the inner primordial material of everything corporeal, and would have to emerge everywhere if the outer potency could only be taken away.

In even the most corporeal of things there lies a point of transfiguration that is often almost sensibly perceptible; without the presence of such a point, even transition from the inorganic to the organic would be inconceivable. Whoever has an eye somewhat practiced in free consideration knows that things do not seem fully completed by what constitutes their existence in the strictest sense; something else in and around them first grants them the full sparkle and shine of life. There is always an overflow, as it were, playing and streaming around .them, an essence that, though indeed intangible [ungreifliches], is not for that matter unremarkable [unbemerkliches]. But this essence that shines through everything – is this not just that inner spiritual matter which still lies concealed in all things of this world, only awaiting its liberation? Among the most corporeal things, metals in particular have always been regarded as individual sparks of light from this essence, glimmering in the darkness of matter. A universal instinct divined the presence of this essence in gold, which seemed most closely related to the spiritual-corporeal essence by virtue of its more passive qualities, its almost infinite ductility, its softness and tenderness, which render it so similar to flesh and result in the greatest indestructibility. Even in one of those seemingly haphazard associations that we so often have the opportunity to observe, all peoples have used gold to symbolize the happy age of the world of innocence and the concord of all things, just as if it were itself yet another sign from that blessed, primordial time.

No age has entirely suppressed the inexorable drive to become master of that inner essence, and this might serve as a proof of how familiar the idea of this essence is to all natural thinking. Let us abandon the usual representation of alchemy to the masses; the alchemists themselves understood what they wanted – never gold, but rather the gold of gold, as it were, or what makes gold into gold. If matter is drawn to the dark essence only through the effect of an outer potency, then there must be another potency opposed to the first. Through this second potency, if it were to fall into human hands, the effect of the outer force could be either canceled or in fact transcended to a particular grade. Now, all matter can only be one as concerns its inner essence, and the difference between corporeal things of the same level might be based only on the greater or lesser influence of the coagulating potency. Accordingly, under this presupposition it would indeed be possible, through a gradual transcendence of this force, to transform the less noble metals stepwise into nobler ones, and finally into the noblest (although this would be only a very subordinate application of a far more general faculty). Our present concern is not to investigate what that other potency could be, whether it is the original-spiritual essence of matter itself or yet another potency altogether (although it is a well-known law that only the free are able to free others). But this much is clear: a metamorphosis of this sort (however it might occur) would always be based on the possibility of returning some degree of mutual freedom and independence to the inner forces of matter, a freedom and independence that has been withdrawn from them by the outer potency and that we have recognized as their original condition.

Accordingly, this essence seems so close to being reproduced in organic nature, particularly in the animal kingdom. If that point of transfiguration which lies in all matter actually arises anywhere, it is in the organic creature, which apparently distinguishes itself from the inorganic only by opening up this essence at a higher level. For here, this incorporeal essence is almost sensibly visible. It is the oil that replenishes the green of plants; it is recognizable in the way that flesh and the eyes shine forth, in that undeniable physical effluence through which the presence of the pure, the healthy, and the loving benefits and liberates us. The essence that emanates as grace [Anmuth] in the highest transfiguration of human corporeality is universally regarded as spiritual; yet even this cannot be thought in the absence of a physically active something, which alone renders explicable the involuntary delight or wonder with which the gaze is filled and which even the barbarian cannot hold back.

Concerning the ordered succession of elements that steadily goes out from nature into eternity, we can ⟨thus⟩[1] maintain: matter below, spirit above – or turned toward eternity. Spirit can be free with respect to eternity, because it has its own root, independent of eternity. It thus turns freely toward eternity and posits itself in immediate connection to eternal being, thereby lifting itself above matter and becoming free with respect to matter as well, and freely creative and active in it.

Spirit cannot pull this being of eternity to itself without thereby positing it as active being[2] in relation to what-eternally-is, thereby making a division in eternity, and finally also moving that very innermost principle, the still concealed expressing of eternity, to action.

Now we must consider and explain all of this in its particulars.

Spirit, we have said, becomes freely creative in matter through its connection to the Eternal. This is how things stand with it. Matter, or the material that is passive toward spirit, is a product of opposing forces that are naturally inclined to strive together to control each other. Because of their natural yearning to be one, these forces constantly strive to cancel their opposition. But spirit can only arise in its freedom as a living unity when these forces are divided and separated from each other. It is therefore in the nature of spirit to insist constantly on division. But because this division can never be complete, and a certain unity always remains as the forces disperse, a view [Blick] of unity rises out of the division. Due to its purity, this view goes to eternity where it appears as a circumscribed, bounded, and, as it were, spiritual image of a creation.

But because spirit stands in connection to eternal being, it works freely against matter, not blindly and insensibly, to disperse the forces.

---

[1] [*Marginal correction by Schelling's son:* accordingly.]
[2] As object.

Eternal being is nothing other than the eternal ectype [Gegen-bildliches] or what is objective of God. Accordingly, it contains in an eternal manner everything that will one day be objectively actual by virtue of God's being. But it only contains this in an unexpressed manner, or in terms of its possibility. Now that the spirit of nature wants to be the link between eternity and nature, it strives to express actually in matter – as material that is subordinated to it – what is contained only as possibility in eternal being. Spirit does so in order to hold [this actualization] up to eternal being (which in itself is pure spirit) as if in a mirror, and thereby pull this being to itself and out of its eternal indifference.

But through just this pulling-toward, eternal being is at the same time pulled away from what-eternally-is and becomes an actual counterpoint [Gegenwurf] for it, in which what-eternally-is can perceive everything. Since what-eternally-is sees into the eternal being, the images of future things that arise in eternal being are revealed to it as well, and so these images indirectly reach up to the highest subject. In this state, everything that will one day be actual in nature passed before what-eternally-is. For the creative spirit ran through the entire ladder of formations ⟨up to the sweet and blessed figure of man⟩, treating matter[1] as a material for its free pleasure, not working blindly, but rather taking as patterns the possibilities or spirits of things that it sees in eternal being, in order to make them corporeal and thus to unfold a complete image of the future world. But all this passed before the eye of the Eternal only as a view or vision [Gesicht]; as a view, because it only viewed [aufblickte] the delicate medium, as it were; as a vision, because no sooner had it arisen than it passed away; and nothing was enduring, nothing was solid, but everything was in unceasing formation. For the confirming and the truly expressing word was still missing.

In this state, what is objective of eternity had a twofold relation in general. On the one hand, it was pulled toward nature as immediately what-is for nature, as its spirit and its subject. But on the other hand, upward[2] or toward what-eternally-is, it acted as a counterpoint and as the immediate nature of what-eternally-is,

---

[1] Opposition.

[2] [*Translator's note:* reading *nach* for *noch.*]

so to speak. Just as eternal being is pulled by nature, eternal being likewise pulls what-eternally-is to itself, [acting as] its immediate nature, and wants nothing other than to be actually posited by what-eternally-is, as its own being. Eternal being too makes itself material in relation to what-eternally-is. In eternal being too, the inner forces are awakened through the pulling-toward of what is below. In it too, a spirit produces itself that sees into the being of eternity, just as the spirit of nature sees into eternal being. Through this spirit, eternal being also recognizes the possibilities contained in what lies innermost, in the authentic subject of God. And since it wants to pull what-eternally-is to itself and move it to posit itself as immediately and actually what-is for *eternal being*, eternal being too seeks to present as actual those possibilities contained within it in an unexpressed manner, and to show to the Eternal as if in a mirror the most concealed thoughts of what lies innermost within its own self, thoughts that it itself does not know.

And so the Eternal saw for the first time, in the immediate ectype of its essence, everything that will one day be in nature, whereupon it saw in just this the deepest thoughts of what lies innermost within its own self; for these rose out from it as spirits, exhibited and actualized in eternal being as if in material; and the view of these spirits, due to its purity, ascended to the highest subject.

The visions of these very innermost thoughts of God that arise actualized from eternal being were nothing other than the visions of future spirits whose creation was determined at the same time as that of natural things. To the extent that it became material or assumed passive qualities toward what-eternally-is, eternal being was itself nothing other than the material or foundation for the future world of spirits. For just as no creation is conceivable without a definite foundation, no creation of spirits is possible either, except from an actual, available material. It might seem outrageous to common conceptions, but it is nonetheless true that precisely what is objective of eternity – which is destined to be the immediate subject of nature – was at the same time the material or matter for (what from the present standpoint is) the still future world of spirits.

Language maintains a strict distinction between nature and the world of spirits by calling the latter quite simply *eternity*. Accordingly, someone who passes over into the world of spirits is said to have gone to eternity. Through this locution, language characterizes nature as somehow having a beginning – and indeed it does, in a certain sense, in comparison with eternity. For nature was not present in the original eternity; rather, it was first presented as a companion to eternity by a productive – though eternal – force. On the other hand, what we view as the foundation (the substrate) of the world of spirits was already present in the unbeginning eternity; it was eternally near God and with God (whateternally-is), and we can thus understand the saying that serves piety so well, that the pious will go to God when they die. For if God were understood as what-eternally-is, such a transition without destruction of character (individuality) would be unimaginable. Similarly, if spirits were created from what-is of God, or were mere forms of it, there would be nothing between God and spirits through which they could be distinguished. It would consequently be impossible for spirits to have a freedom with respect to God. Anything that has a freedom with respect to God must come from a ground independent of him; and even if something is originally and in a narrower sense *in* God, it must come from something (or have something as a foundation and principle of differentiation) other than God himself, although it is within him. Thus, the existence of a world of spirits presupposes something that is eternally within or by God without itself being God.

In this way, a steady succession of elements develops, reaching from what is uppermost to the undermost, connecting the lowest with the highest of all.

With this it becomes evident that this entire internally thriving, vibrant state is based on the mutual freedom and independence of the constitutive elements with respect to each other.[1] The spirit that rises from below acts as an intermediating essence; and if it were not free with respect to eternity, it could not enter into a free, active relation with eternal being, nor could it hold up to eternal being as if in a reflection [Widerschein] the pos-

[1] [*Marginal note:* ⟨is based *rather* on the fact that ⟨A^3⟩ x is still free from A^2⟩.]

sibilities that eternal being contains. But if the attraction of nature did not render eternal being likewise free and active with respect to what-is, then eternal being could not show it, as if in a vision, either the images of the things that will one day be actual in nature or the miracle of its own essence, the thoughts of what lies innermost within itself, the future spirits. This contemplative life, this inner clarity would be immediately canceled if the freedom that the elements have with respect to each other were to be canceled.

We will attempt to elucidate this situation by way of its similarity to human nature. Everything divine is human, according to Hippocrates, and everything human is divine. If so, we can hope to approach the truth by relating everything to man.

In organic nature, the immediate communication between the physical and the spiritual first reemerges with the mutual unfolding and independence of the forces.[1] This communication, which has so often taxed human ingenuity, can be satisfactorily explained only through the insight that matter, while capable of passive or even corporeal qualities when facing outward or downward, is nonetheless spiritual in itself and facing upward. The same is evident in humans; what proves corporeal when facing downward is in fact spiritual when facing upward, or on the side turned toward spirit. It emanates a spiritual essence, which here too presents itself as the link between eternity and time. Through the process of life itself, an image and inner life-spirit constantly arises from the corporeal, a life-spirit that through this very process is constantly re-embodied. Here too, a spirit arising from below is an intermediating essence through which the undermost might reach the uppermost, and the lowest is able to enter[2] into connection with the highest.

Just as we cannot explain the present corporeal state of matter by reference to its interior, but rather only as the effect of an outer potency; likewise, man (like all organic things) seems at least partly subject to an outer potency that cancels the free relation of

[1] [*Marginal note:* ⟨There are states of human nature in which the Highest becomes free. Sleep. But as a rule in visions and likewise in the exceptional states.⟩]

[2] [*Translator's note:* reading *treten* for *reten.*]

forces within him and transforms the relation into a necessary one.[1]

Internally, a waking man and a sleeping man are entirely the same. None of the inner forces that are active in the waking state are lost in sleep. From this it is already evident that the difference between these states, as well as their alternation, is not determined from within the organism; rather, it is the effect of a potency *external* to the organism, now attracting, now releasing. All forces of a man in the waking state are apparently governed by a unity that holds them together like a common exponent (or expressing), as it were. In sleep, by contrast, each force and each instrument seems to work for itself,[2] and a freely willed sympathy takes the place of an externally determined unity. And while the whole looks as though it were dead and ineffective on the outside, the freest play and intercommunication of forces seems to unfold on the inside.

In the normal course of life, the effect of that outer force of attraction appears as sometimes waning, sometimes disruptive, in regular alternation. When this happens, an unusual suspension or weakening of this force seems possible, according to the familiar phenomena of so-called animal magnetism. Indeed, the power seems actually given to one man to transcend that outer potency and return another man to the free inner relations of life, so that he appears dead externally, while internally a steady and free connection of all forces emerges from the lowest up to the highest.

For many reasons, it seems to me that mesmeric sleep is much too strictly differentiated from normal sleep. For since we have only very vague reports of the inner processes of normal sleep, nothing proves that these processes are not similar or even equal to those of mesmeric sleep; and we would not learn about the processes of mesmeric sleep either, if it were not for the particular connection of the mesmerized to those who put them into this

---

[1] [*Marginal note added by Schelling's son:* ⟨The violence of that eternal potency is manifest, not only to the extent that it holds fast to the organic in general as something corporeal, but in a higher potency still, in that externalization of the inner life which occurs in the waking state.⟩]

[2] [*Marginal note:* ⟨that One also lifts itself up again⟩.]

state. We know that the inner events of mesmeric sleep are not always similar, even to each other: there are gradations of mesmeric sleep. There is a level at which it cannot be distinguished from normal sleep, and there is another at which man seems completely cut off from the sensuous world and entirely removed to a spiritual realm. Since we distinguish grades of depth as well as intensity in normal sleep, we cannot know which gradations of mesmeric sleep might not also be reached by normal sleep.

It is a well-known fact that the ancients already distinguished between two sorts of dreams, of which only one sort was considered divine. We wish to distinguish between dreams that originate out of the mutual independence of the inner forces, and those that originate from their dependence. We will disregard dreams of the latter description. We can assume three gradations among those of the first type. The lowest gradation would be one in which the life-spirit, that intermediating essence between body and spirit, would attract what is objective of the soul. By means of this [objective aspect], the life-spirit would then become free with respect to the body in order either to act as a healing force, removing the existing disorder in the body, or to reveal to the soul those [disorders] of the body that lie concealed. A higher gradation would be one in which[1] this very life-spirit attracts what is objective of the soul, but this time in order to show it what lies within its own self, as if in a counterpoint, and to bring to it knowledge of what is still wrapped up in itself and awaiting the future. At this level, there would already be a free relation between what is eternal of the soul and the spirit that arises from below. Through this relation, spirit becomes both an instrument of, and a slate for, this higher principle, a slate on which this higher principle is able to read what lies concealed within itself. Finally, the highest stage would be one[2] in which the process of freedom spreads up to what is eternal of the soul itself, within which alone free communication takes place between what is eternally objective and what is eternally subjective of the soul. Here, what-is of the soul would become free even from its own eternal being, and would be put in a relation to this

[1] [*Marginal note:* A[2] and A[3].]
[2] A[3] and x.

159

being such that it could, so to speak, distinguish and read its deepest thoughts in this latter. The potency that binds the Eternal to what lies below and to the world of senses would be transcended; the soul would be transported to the otherworldly realm, and, as it were, entirely to the world of spirits.

It is possible that these gradations could actually be detected in mesmeric sleep. Normal sleep may well vary considerably according to person and context, but those dreams that correspond to the higher grades of intensity would indisputably act very much like the visions [Visionen] of mesmeric sleep, of which no memory is retained in the waking state, and of which we have reports only through the connection mentioned earlier. We entirely fail to recall many dreams in the waking state. This fact can be accepted as certain, since we are certain through experience that many dreams leave only the general memory of having-been-there, and that others vanish just after waking and can often be retained only at the moment of waking (and sometimes even then not permanently). It is just possible that the more external dreams often mirror the more internal dreams, and that in this manner internal dreams can come immediately to consciousness, although confusedly and not in their pure and complete condition.[1]

If we may now apply this back to an earlier discussion, we can imagine it to be at least possible that men are entitled to a similar violence against other earthly things as they seem in part to be

---

[1] [*Marginal note added by Schelling's son*: However it is understood, in mesmeric sleep we have the example of a state in which there is, externally, no subject at all, and yet there is an inner subject who judges, concludes, thinks and comprehends, often considerably exceeding his normal capacity, and is fully alive and operational. This state is living proof of that result which the first observer – roughly but not incorrectly – termed "dis-organized" (Entorganisiren): in other words, a sublation of the outer unity of the organism, against which the inner unity rises up in full freedom. Disease is only possible to the extent that all forces and organs of life are subjugated to a common exponent, whereby the individual is sacrificed to the whole and must follow in a direction that is inappropriate for it or against its nature. Accordingly, I can understand the healing power of a state in which the individual force, temporarily freed from the chain of the whole, gains time to reestablish itself in its integrity and originality.

allowed against other men. They would then be in a position, through an entirely similar effect, to set free the interior of other corporeal things up to a particular grade, and thereby initiate true transformations through which a set of phenomena could emerge, phenomena that would be entirely different from those of normal experiments, which, however deeply they may penetrate, still only play on the surface.

⟨So much[1]⟩ for the explanation of that inner state of pure contemplation in which ⟨the Eternal⟩[2] perceives, as if in a vision, the miracles of[3] time ⟨and eternity⟩.

The original meaning of the word *Idea,* [Idea] which we have so felicitously inherited, is actually no different from that of the German word for *vision* [Gesicht]. Indeed, both words mean two things, denoting as much a view [Blick] as what is viewed.

The doctrine of the archetypes of things is lost in deepest antiquity; the Greeks already regarded it as a sacred legacy. This certainly fosters the suspicion that the doctrine had lost something of its original meaning by then, since even Plato was only a reporter and interpreter of this ancient teaching. Later on, the true meaning became obscured in several ways; first it was understood far too supernaturally, and then in an entirely vulgar sense. The production of such archetypes or visions of future things is a necessary moment in the overall development of life, and even if these archetypal images cannot be understood as physical natures in precisely the normal sense, they certainly cannot be thought apart from all physicality. They are neither merely universal concepts of the understanding, nor fixed models; for they are Ideas precisely because they are eternally full of life, in ceaseless motion and production.

We said that the production of such archetypes is a necessary moment; but after this moment they neither pass away, nor stay as they are. Rather, the moment itself eternally remains, because each following moment holds fast to its predecessor. These archetypes still stream out from the innermost part of creative nature, just as fresh and alive as they were before time. Nature still ap-

[1] Only this.
[2] The eternal time.
[3] Future.

pears visionary [Visionär] although, in a certain sense, it acts blindly. For even if nature is guided by the light of a higher understanding, how could it grasp and comprehend this understanding? Without this visionary quality, so much that is undeniably teleological and intentional (in both the whole of nature and in its parts) and that can already be found in nature's first designs, would be entirely lacking explanation; and both the general and particular technicism of nature would be incomprehensible. No entity to this day can be created without the repeated production of its archetype. Indeed, we will hazard the assertion that every act of generation occurring in nature marks a return to a moment of the past, a moment that is allowed for an instant to enter the present time as an alienated (re)appearance. For, since time commences absolutely in each living thing, and since at the beginning of each life time is connected to eternity anew, then an eternity must immediately precede each life. The return of a moment of the past in each act of generation could even lend credence to physical appearances: there is a disruption of forces, a relaxation of all links, and being is posited-outside-itself. It is as if the external link had been momentarily abolished (perhaps because it had the highest grade of attraction.[1]) And here too, it is as if a guiding connection and a chain of mutually independent elements were established whereby the first element becomes capable of effecting the last, just as the father undeniably begets [einzeugt] the character and disposition of the child. This explanation accounts for the similarity of generation with death, as well as with the phenomena of mesmeric sleep. And if an organic entity or human being can be subjected to pain (in both the physical as well as the psychic sense) only by the power of the external life-exponent, then it is entirely conceivable how, with the suspension of that exponent, a complete absence of pain and that feeling of bliss – of which the previously mentioned states [i.e., generation and mesmeric sleep] are full – can emerge. And it is conceivable how a sudden and momentary suspension of that exponent showers us with the highest degree of pleasure.

Yet we hardly dare touch the veil that has been pulled over these great mysteries; we fear that we will either be misun-

[1] Negation.

derstood, or that we will ourselves err in the details and fail to express ourselves correctly, since all the phenomena we have identified have such a multitude of facets and branch off in all directions. If we one day succeed in continuing this history up to the time and to the manifold conditions of which the human life consists and under which it persists, then we will certainly find many things to amend or present in a higher light.

We might pose one more question to help clarify our thoughts. Why do all great doctrines so unanimously call upon man to divide himself from himself, and give him to understand that he would be able to do anything and could effect all things if he only knew to free his higher self from his subordinate self? It is a hindrance for man to be posited-in-himself; he is capable of higher things only to the extent that he is able to posit himself out of himself – to the extent that he can become *posited-outside-himself* [außer-sich-gesetzt], as our language so marvelously expresses. And we also clearly understand (still considering only spiritual forms of production), how an ever higher, free, inner contact takes place according to the different gradations of spiritual productions, and how the same thing is required everywhere. [This is the case, to be sure,] unless what is eternal of the soul is in immediate contact with its own being (and is thus contained entirely in itself); or unless there is contact between the Eternal and some demon that accompanies it, a genius that nature has given us as a companion, and that alone is capable of serving as an instrument to being, to the extent that the conscious spirit lifts itself above the genius. And just as the inner freedom of the mind conditions all spiritual production, we see by comparison that men always prove less capable of true, spiritual production to the extent that they are or are becoming unfree.

The peoples of the Orient have clearly recognized a playful pleasure at the beginning of the life of God, which they have eloquently termed Wisdom;[1] it is an unblemished mirror of divine force and (due to passive qualities) an image of his benevolence. With astonishing precision, they everywhere ascribed more of a passive than an active nature to this essence. For this reason, they did not call it, ⟨as we have been doing, the⟩ spirit; nor

---

[1] [*Marginal note:* as they represent it as a gleam of the eternal light.]

did they call it ⟨the⟩ Word (or ⟨the⟩ Logos), although wisdom was later often (incorrectly) confused with this term. Rather, they ascribed a feminine name to it, by which they meant to suggest that this essence is only passive and receptive, in contrast to the higher essence.

Language in a book that is rightly considered divine drifts over us like a fresh morning breeze from the holy dawn of the world, language that introduces Wisdom in speech. The Lord possessed me in the beginning of his way, before he did anything. I was set up from eternity, from the beginning, or ever the earth was. When there were no depths, I was brought forth; when there were no fountains abounding[1] water. Before the mountains were settled, before the hills am I brought forth. When he prepared the heavens above, I was there: when he set a compass upon the face of the depth; when he appointed the foundations [Grund] of the earth, then I was by him, ⟨as one brought up with him⟩: and I was daily his pleasure, playing always ⟨by⟩[2] him.[3]

With these words, Wisdom is sharply distinguished from the Lord. The Lord possessed Wisdom, but she was not herself the Lord.[4] She was with him ⟨before the⟩[5] beginning,[6] before he did anything. ⟨We say⟩[7] that a man does nothing if he is sleeping, or

[1] With.

[2] Before.

[3] I rejoiced in the habitable part of his earth; and my delights *were* with the sons of men. [*Translator's note:* this paragraph is comprised of quotations (faithful, for the most part) from Luther's translation of Proverbs 8:22–31, excluding 8:26 and 8:28.]

[4] [*Marginal note:* The Lord was he with whom all power and all force resided, that resting will that did not yet will. For precisely this reason, spirit was inexpressible; the primordial language, here as elsewhere, called it by that inexpressible name (Jehovah), that which is absolutely and always One. On the other hand, the primordial language reserves the name *Elohim* for the divine essence that encompasses in itself the majority of forces (the immediate subject of that One).]

[5] In the.

[6] [*Marginal note:* or as the beginning of his way, that is, as the beginning of his always progressing (never regressing) workings, before he emerged from himself, as it were.]

[7] The German language now says.

dead, or enraptured – if, in short, he does not manifest himself as a thing-that-is. Wisdom is compared to a child: a child can be called self-less when, in the earliest time, all of its inner forces work with each other,[1] but without a will having come forth to hold them together and make itself their collective force and unity. ⟨Wisdom, together with the first corporeality in which she is clad, is like a tranquil, passive unity that cannot lift itself up from a merely germinal state into a state of activity.⟩[2]

But just as times of innocence do not last, and the games of childhood that serve as patterns for future life are transitory, the blessed dream of the gods likewise cannot remain. All merely germinal life is of itself full of longing; it increasingly demands to emerge from mute, ineffective unity and to be lifted instead into an active unity. In the same way, we see the whole of nature to be equally full of longing; the earth sucks the force of heaven into itself through countless mouths; the seed strives toward light and air, in order to catch sight of an image, a spirit; the flower sways in the sun's rays in order to pull them into itself as color. And the same holds true for that ⟨passive⟩[3] life: the more it unfolds, the more it calls upon the invisible to accept it, pull it in, and recognize it as its own. Forsaken, Wisdom laments the lot of her creatures, that the children of her pleasure do not remain, but rather ⟨stand⟩[4] in perpetual struggle and through this struggle pass

---

[1] And are excited by gentle interplay.

[2] [*Marginal note:* So too, that first essence is still self- and will-less, and all unity, all inclination that the forces have to each other, is only for pleasure and not in earnest, it is only play and not a deed through which alone it could come to something solid and enduring. Wisdom played in the sight of the Lord, upon his earth (Erdboden), upon that which is ground (Grund) and soil (Boden) to the Lord, that first living and resting place of all creatures. And even in this early time, Wisdom's pleasure was the creation that was destined to one day produce the link between matter and the world of spirits, and to be immediately receptive to Wisdom, although mediately receptive to the bright divinity. Thus, Wisdom played before the Lord, filled with childlike presentiment, and he saw in her what will one day be, as if it were a golden future in a youthful dream.

[3] Playful.

[4] Are.

away again. But longing draws near, and the invisible too is thereby drawn to the visible.

Wisdom was by the Lord. But who is the *Lord?* Indisputably, he is that will which rests *within* being and what-is, the will through which alone being can actually be being and what-is can actually be what-is: the will that previously willed nothing. This is the Lord, for all power and all force come from him, or *he* is the expressing of all essence.[1] *He* is being and what-is and is inseparable from both. What happens to them concerns him as well, and if they are drawn out of indifference, he himself cannot remain indifferent either. It was only because they were at rest that he did not pull them to himself. Now that both have been put into motion, he is necessarily summoned into action as well. If being is drawn toward nature, it is his own being which is so drawn; or rather, he first recognizes it as his own when it is drawn. If what-is, is summoned to posit itself actually as such in relation to being, he himself is drawn out of indifference, for he is the expressing of what-is. In this very summoning, he thus recognizes what-is as his own, as that of which he is the expressing.

For this reason, those ancient words rightly say: the Lord had Wisdom, she played before him, he saw in her what will one day be; ⟨for what is true of being and of what-is, is also true of the Lord.⟩ This is because being and what-is are the being of the Lord, and what-is of the Lord. ⟨Or put succinctly,⟩ in just this moment, in the movement posited through the attraction of nature, ⟨they become, and⟩ he recognizes them as his being and what-is, and himself as the *Lord*, as the expressing of both.

We can easily observe that it is not sufficient for a man's complete actuality that he merely be something or implicitly have something. In addition, he needs to become aware of what he is and what he has. He is a thing-that-is, and he has a being by nature, without any effort, even as a child. But both this thing-that-he-is and this being [that he has] are ineffective until a force

[1] He is different from being and what-is but is not separated from them. He is the will that is now still inactive, through which alone both can become active. He did not attract them and did not actually make them active, because, as pure willing, no ground for action lay in him; and neither of the opposites were able to awake him, because they themselves were at rest.

is found that is independent of both, that becomes aware of them both and activates them. It is not enough that forces (or abilities) be present in a man; he must recognize them as his own, and only then is it possible for him to grasp onto them and put them to work and into effect.

It can likewise be said of the will of eternity – which has remained at rest until now – that this moment, the moment when it becomes aware of what it is, is the moment of awakening, of coming-to-itself in the true sense. This will was not added to being or to what-is, as something foreign to them; rather, it was in them from eternity and simply did not externalize itself. So the will does not happen upon anything foreign, it comes upon its self, upon what it was before eternity, and of which it was merely not aware.

This was the highest goal . . .[1] [The will] must become aware [of what-is, and of being], must recognize them as its own, and only then can it lay hold of them and in so doing, become fully itself.

We can say of the expressing – which used to be an indifferent will – that this moment, the moment when it becomes aware of what it is, is the moment of awakening, of coming-to-itself in the true sense. This, then, is the highest goal of that activity which came up from below, ⟨in which it comes to a halt⟩. This is the final effect of the entire process we have been describing – an effect to which everything else, even those visions of future things, has only served as a means.

Everything has happened only so that what was concealed – namely, the expressing of what-is and of being – becomes aware of this thing-that-is, and of this being, as its self. But it cannot recognize itself as what-is, and as being, without at the same time recognizing nature as its own, previously unconscious, longing for its self, a longing ⟨that it hitherto did not know⟩.

We thus see everything ready for a decision; and for the Eternal, this last stage in which it becomes aware of itself marks the boundary between the past state and the one to follow.

[1] [*Translator's note:* According to the German editor, the printed manuscript ends here, and the rest of page 109 remains blank. What follows is a variant of page 109 and the further continuation from the typeset proofs.]

The unity that we have considered up until now was mute and ineffective. Yet all the forces were in blissful interaction. This was the case first in the forces of nature, but this action was not itself expressed and posited again *as active*. The forces merely *were* in that action, but not *as* being in that action. There was merely a framework for an action, just as when the forces inside of us incline toward some operation or production, but the decision [Entschluß] that puts the action into effect is not present. The situation was the same with what-eternally-is, and with the being of eternity; being was indeed summoned, and it was ready to posit itself as what immediately affirms nature. But it was ready only inwardly and not outwardly – only according to intent, but not according to deed. Likewise, what-is was already what-is – to the extent that it was summoned to posit itself as such – and yet it was not what-is, because it had not actually posited itself as such.

Accordingly, eternal being feels itself drawn to the originary [will] and clearly wants to be what immediately affirms it; likewise what-is is drawn to both [being and the will] and demands to be what affirms both in common. But precisely in being so drawn, the will that wills nothing becomes perceptible to them as their force and their expressing. Thus, they both will and do not will. They will to the extent that they were drawn and summoned, but they do not will because they do not want to leave the will that wills nothing, which in just this moment becomes perceptible to them as the Lord, as he in whom all force subsists.

But even if they were neither able nor willing to decide straightaway, they were indeed drawn to decide. Actual opposition is thereby generated, and they thereby become perceptible to the will that wills nothing. As long as the opposition remained dormant, [the will] remained in its indifference and did not know [the opposition]. Now the opposition is put to work and is made perceptible to the will that wills nothing, which is now pulled into action, becoming an actual will, whereas it was previously a merely possible will. But it can only become actual as what it is. Once and for all, it is impossible for any thing to be sublated. The will can therefore only become actual as the will *that wills nothing*. But since it was previously a resting will that specifically did not will anything positive, and it is now summoned to express what-is and to express being *as* what-is and *as* being, it becomes from[1] itself the will that positively wills nothing, not even itself as what-is and as being. That is, it becomes the will that opposes to itself the particularity, dispersion, and mutual freedom of the principles.

In the meantime, there were from the very beginning two different though not distinguishable aspects of the will that willed nothing. First, it was pure will in itself; but as such, it was also the will that willed nothing. Now only this second aspect has become a positively negating will; besides this, it still remains a pure will, and this quality of being a will cannot be destroyed. It is even impossible that another, opposed, will not produce itself in it, to the extent that it remains a will, and precisely because it became a positively negating will. This opposed will is one that actually wills itself as what-is, and as being; it is, in a word, an affirming will, a will of love that does not will nothing but rather wills[2] something.[3]

It is thus now the case that one and the same will = *x* is two wills: one determinately negating and the other affirming. These two wills cannot act as two parts of one will, since it is wholly and indivisibly the will that positively wills nothing. It can therefore be the willing will only wholly and indivisibly.

With this, the highest contradiction finally emerges. For there are not two inactive wills here, nor is one of the two inactive; rather, both are active. One and the same will is activated as the will that wills nothing and is also activated as the will that wills something (life and actuality). Because the highest contradiction is necessarily also the highest movement of life, it can thus be seen here and from the outset that an absolute decision is demanded.

But when two conflicting wills are present – one affirming and one negating – spirit is already called for as well. Or rather, spirit is present according to possibility and should emerge but cannot, because it is the free unity of both wills, but a unity is impossible.

[1] [*Translator's note:* reading *von* for *vor.*]
[2] [*Marginal note:* It is impossible for the will (which is now a will that positively wills nothing) not to be called upon by that which is nothing without it, and which can only be lifted into a state of activity by it.]
[3] ⟨everything⟩.

169

We can therefore see that in the very moment when the Highest is supposed to express itself, it becomes the inexpressible. Let no one be mistaken about this, or waste time in debate against those who deny it. One must in fact insist on this very inexpressibility, because it is necessary for the highest life. If what wills to express itself in all life were not inexpressible by nature, how would there be any vital motion? How would there be an impulse toward expressibility, articulation, or organic relation? And moreover, without this, how would there be an absolutely Highest that never becomes the expressible, but eternally remains only the expressing? For in precisely this inexpressibility – where it is not to be said that the Eternal is the will that wills nothing, nor that the Eternal is the will that wills, nor that it is the unity of both – in just this inexpressibility, something *which is none of them,* the pure I of divinity, becomes actual and ascends in the inaccessible glare of its purity ⟨which no created thing may approach⟩. Everyone can now see how we have only gradually reached the point where we might recognize this I of divinity in its ⟨complete purity and⟩ inexpressibility; how would you sense or recognize it without gradually ascending to it?

It is apparent that none of these – not the negating, not the affirming will, and not the merely potentially extant will that is their unity – is that absolute I of divinity as it was before the activation; but precisely because it is *none* of these and yet is all three, precisely thereby it appears as *actual,* as what is in principle inexpressible; ⟨ it appears as what in principle is the inexpressible essence of divinity.⟩

If none of the three is the pure I of divinity, then what are they? It is apparent that they can act toward the divine I only as just so many particular I-hoods. Everyone unanimously calls the deity a being of beings [Wesen aller Wesen]. But it can be this only with respect to the affirming will. Yet there could be no affirming will without the negating will. The affirming will is the will of love, but on its own love does not attain *being.* Being (existence) is individuality and isolation. But love is the nothingness of individuality: it does not seek its own. For this reason, although love in itself is what-is, it cannot *be* (or exist as) this on its own. Likewise, a being of beings [Wesen aller Wesen] does not bear anything; it is in itself the opposite of personality, and it must be provided a ground by the personal I-hood (that rejects the outside). Only the something is the bearer of the nothing, or of that which cannot *be* on its own. But just as a being of beings could not *be* (exist) without a force that opposes love, it likewise could not be the being of beings without a will that resists negation. If the force of individuality were alone, there would be nothing but the eternal state of closing oneself off and being closed off. Nothing could live in this state, created things would be impossible, and the concept of a being of beings would be lost. For this force of self-ness or individuality in God is captured in that barbaric term *aseity* [Aseität]. This force is the white heat of purity, intensified to a fiery glare by the pull of nature. It is unapproachable, unbearable to all created things, and would rage against every creature like ruinous fire, an eternal wrath that tolerates nothing, fatally contracting but for the resistance of love.

But whoever acknowledges duality must also admit triplicity. The pure I of divinity *is* each of these three, not in itself, but only to the extent that it is persuaded and is eternally being persuaded actually to express itself.

At the present moment, however, the conflicting wills balance each other out. Indeed, the will that is both must absolutely be entirely the one or entirely the other, either entirely affirmation or entirely negation, entirely love or wrath. It is in precisely this way that the very highest freedom emerges. Unconditioned freedom is not a characteristic of particular actions; it is rather the capacity to be entirely one or entirely the other of two contradictory things.

To state the terms of the conflict as precisely as possible, the relationship is the following: one will wants the essence (what-is and being) to remain closed and hence concealed, just as it was before. The other will wants the essence to open up and abandon its concealment.

How is a decision possible here? Perhaps someone might say that one of the wills is by nature subservient to the other, in which case it would necessarily be overcome by the other will, and this other would then be the victor. But this presupposition is false. Both wills are by nature equally important, each has the same right to be active, and it is necessarily true that neither retreats before the other. But all this must be the case if God is to appear as the freest essence of all, if a necessary origin of the world is to be revealed rather than discovered, and if all that there is, exists only by virtue of the free, divine will.

If there were no contradiction then there would be no freedom. In the strain of the forces, when life hangs in the balance [auf der Spitze], as it were, only the deed can decide; for the two wills cannot be prized apart by natural necessity. By virtue of natural necessity alone, the wills would instead eternally remain in that intentional state, since neither can emerge before the other. If they are not to be prized apart by necessity, they must be separated by free will. But how is active freedom possible? How is decision possible?

The conflicting wills are certainly not bound to each other. If, in the expressible, the relation between the opposites is characterized by an inner necessity compelling them to be one (because both are equally necessary to the whole) – then, in the expressing, the relation between the forces is characterized by an inner freedom not to be one, but rather for each to be for itself. Each of the wills is individual and self-sufficient, and each has the complete freedom to posit itself and to negate the other. But precisely because they are equally unconditioned, neither will can negate the other without being negated by it in turn; and similarly the other way around: neither can posit itself without also positing the other.

How is a decision possible here, even only with respect to the What? A decision is hampered by the absolute parity (equipollence) of both wills, by the fact that neither has more of a claim to be active than the other. If one were active, then the other could certainly be as well. The only impossible state of affairs would be for one to be active when the other is not, since that *would* conflict with the equipollence. Accordingly, one cannot be insofar as the other is not; on the contrary, if it is, then the other is as well. This is the requirement that emerges from their equipollence. But up until this point we have been viewing the wills according to a relation of contradiction, where precisely the opposite is the case. [The relation of contradiction entails that] if

172

one is active, then the other is not. But since, according to the presupposition, they should indeed each be active, this relation of contradiction must be abandoned. Another relation, a *grounding relation* [Verhältnis des Grundes] must take its place. [This grounding relation is such that] when the one is active, then – precisely for that reason – the other is as well; in other words, one acts only as the ground, the predecessor of the other. Accordingly, with regard to the What, a decision could only consist in a sublation of simultaneity, or the fact that both would be posited in *a single result*.

However, this grounding relation cannot be of the sort where the predecessor [vorangehende] is sublated when the successor [folgende] is posited. Rather, it is of the sort where, when the successor is posited, the predecessor is as well, although it remains only *as a predecessor.* In this way, they would only be in *different potencies* – which can be seen also as different times [verschiedene Zeiten] – though at the same time [zumal]. The preceding will would act as the ground of its successor, and hence as the first potency. Now it could certainly fail to be active in the potency of the other will, but this does not stop it from being all the while as active in *its* potency as the other is in *the other's* potency.

The principle of contradiction comes with the familiar qualification that the same thing cannot be both something and its opposite *at the same time.* Because of the indeterminacy demonstrated earlier, we can in no way approve of this formulation; but the added qualification is particularly inadmissible for a number of reasons. First and foremost, the principle of contradiction should be strictly adhered to, and what this formulation expresses negatively must instead be affirmed, as in the principle of sufficient reason [Satz des Grundes]. [Here we find the claim that] one thing can be something as well as its opposite, if as one thing it is the ground of itself, rather than the ground of something else. But even apart from that, the phrase "at the same time" would be inappropriate, since what exists in different times still exists "at the same time." Only different moments of the same time can be considered successive; or [put another way,] different moments of the same time, regarded as such, cannot be simultaneous. But regarded as different times, they can be "*at the same time.*" Indeed, they are necessarily "at the same time." The past clearly cannot be a present at the same time as the present; but as past, it is certainly simultaneous with the present, and it is easy to see that the same holds true of the future.

Thus, only contradiction at the highest grade of increase is able to break open eternity and disclose the complete system of times. This is *what* would have to occur if a decision were to be made. But the How? is not yet thereby explained.

There can be no doubt concerning which of the two wills should precede and which should follow; it is obvious even in passing, before we have elaborated the fundamental reasoning. The affirming will insists on confrontation, and if it were to precede and the negating will to follow, the process would be reversed, which is unthinkable. This further demonstrates that the negating will, if posited as the expressing of essence, could posit itself only as the ground and predecessor of the other. But does it want to posit itself at all? This has not been addressed up until now. For the negating will can simply deny itself, give up the expressible altogether, and remain by itself in concealment. And precisely this is the only sense in which it can be thought as a negating will, a will that wills a determinate nothing. If it wills *nothing,* it must remain in concealment, not revealing itself anywhere, not even willing of itself [seiner selber wollen]. For only when it does not posit itself does it not posit the other. On the other hand, if it posits itself first, it can (by virtue of the equipollence of both wills) only posit itself as the ground of the other. So the other, the willing or affirming will, is in fact only the will that insists on revelation. Not that it immediately wills itself; rather, it only wills that expression take place at all. For if revelation comes about, this will necessarily also attains the status of being the expressing.

If this is simply the old, seemingly irrepressible opposition between a negating, self-controlling will and an affirming, expansive will, then the first will certainly cannot be forcibly subjugated by the second. Rather, it can only be gently persuaded and amicably convinced to give way to love. Or so we must imagine the course of events, even though this cannot be thought as actually having happened. For it is certainly not *true* that the wills could consult with each other and, as it were, enter into deliberation; all this can only happen in a flash, since it is considered a happening and yet did not actually (explicitly) happen. It is an action that is not decided upon by anyone (for how can something decide when it cannot be?); and yet the will of all [the members] is there, because no one can be forced. It is, in short, an action that can be conceived only on the assumption that [the members have] incomprehensible mutual knowledge and understanding in the inexpressible, which is their unconditioned unity. If you wish to form an image – albeit a vague and distant one – of what occurs, imagine the moment of a sudden need: you have fallen unexpectedly into danger, and, without understanding or deliberation, divine inspiration takes hold and you do the only thing that could save you. Alternatively, to connect this with higher matters – indeed, the only genuinely comparable situation – ask yourself this: did you honestly take factors into consideration, engage in deliberation and reach a decision, when you grasped yourself for the first time and expressed yourself as who you are?

When we speak about the character of a man, we have in mind his distinctiveness, the particularity of what he does and who he is, which is given to him through the expressing of his essence. Men who hesitate to be wholly one thing or another are called characterless; but men are said to have character if they reveal a determinate expressing of their whole essence. Nevertheless, it is a well-known fact that nobody can be given character, and that nobody has chosen for himself the particular character he bears. There is neither deliberation nor choice here, and yet everyone recognizes and judges character as an eternal (never-ceasing, constant) deed and attributes to a man both it as well as the action that follows from it. Universal moral judgment thus acknowledges that every man has a freedom in which there is neither (explicit) deliberation nor choice, a freedom that is itself fate and necessity. But most men shy away from this freedom that opens like an abyss before them, just as they are frightened when faced with the necessity of being wholly one thing or another. They shy away from this as they shy away from everything coming from that inexpressible; and where they see a ray cast by it they turn away as if it were a flash of lightning that brings harm to everything in its way. They feel themselves crushed by this freedom, as by an appearance from an incomprehensible world, from eternity, from a place entirely devoid of any ground at all.

Since there was no time when God could have deliberated with himself and acted, and since only the supreme free will could have decided, it follows that the conflicting wills – the will that insists on the No, as well as the affirming will, and the will that exists only as a possibility (the will of spirit) – these must have been united through an instantaneous, all-illuminating action. This action must have been undeliberated and yet comprehended, an action in which everything was grasped and done in a flash. It was recognized in an instant that if life were not to be lost, the simultaneity of the expressing forces would have to be sublated. And in just this indivisible instant, love swayed the first of the wills standing open. And just as quickly, it was recognized that if one of the two wills were to precede, the only one that could be posited at the beginning was the one that did not will a beginning and that was overcome at that very moment. For there is no beginning without an overcoming, and, for the negating will, preceding was the same as being overcome. Indeed, through a sort of miracle, this was all contained in one and the same indivisible deed, which was at the same time the most freely willed and the most necessary, just as actions occasionally occur that, once finished, no understanding is able to comprehend.

This is the course of the great decision whereby the negating will of the unconditioned I of eternity – or strength and force – was pulled out of concealment and posited at the beginning of the way of God.

We already have had occasion to remark upon a fact that should now strike many, namely that the expressing forces – whose conflict has just been resolved – bear the same relation to each other as did the principles in the originary being of nature. Indeed, we could say that the forces involved in the expressibility of the essence act in precisely the same way as do the expressing forces. The only difference is that the former are posited at the same time and as one, while the latter are posited in succession and as not-one.

Since we now have actually brought nature into unity with eternal being and with what-eternally-is, it is evident that the whole of nature acts as the lowest potency of essence, as the mere ground of existence (A = B). For it has the relation of *being* to the being of eternity, notwithstanding the fact that it contains all potencies in itself. The being of eternity, on the other hand, acts as what-immediately-is of nature, or what immediately affirms nature; it relates to nature as the second potency (= A^2). Finally, since what-is of eternity is summoned to posit itself as what affirms both in common, it would act as what affirms the third potency (= A^3).

But this is the very same relationship as obtained between the expressing powers. Because the negating will is posited as preceding, it is also posited as the *ground* of existence [Existenz], as *being*, as the (A = B) of what is higher. Moreover, the affirming will (which is grounded by the negating will) would act as A^2. Finally, the third – their living unity – would be to them what A^3 is in the expressible. In general, this agreement is not remarkable, for all life involves a Yes and a No; expansive activity and restrictive force are the necessary inner principles of all life. Whatever an essence may be internally, it must be the same thing externally; that is, the same forces that are involved in its inner and expressed life are (by nature) the expressing forces of its existence [Daseyn] as well. But they can manifest themselves as such only successively or with decision. Thus, *the principles of being in simultaneity are the*[1] *potencies of becoming in succession.* Eternity rebounds off the expressing forces. For this reason, if people wish to use the concepts of unity and totality but simply posit unity as totality and do not dare to accept a decision, they will never be able to come out from eternity.

This unanimity of the expressing and the expressed can be found in all life; indeed, every living creature requires such a unanimity if it is to achieve completion and active existence. We find three main forces in the expressed, in what lies within every organism. Through the first force, it is in itself; it constantly produces and maintains itself. Through the second, it strives toward the outside; and to a certain extent, the third unites the characters

[1] [*Translator's note:* reading *die* for *sie.*]

of the other two forces in itself. Each of the forces is necessary to the inner being of the whole, and if any of them were to be taken away, the whole would necessarily be destroyed as well. But this whole is not a resting, static being; once posited as expressible, the essence of the organism immediately goes over to the express-ing. The very forces at work internally emerge (by nature) exter-nally as potencies, and with decision. One force incorporates the others and posits itself as governing, as the common exponent of the whole. Thus following each other, these forces become the determining potencies of the external periods of an organism's life, the times of its becoming and of its development; similarly, when they acted together, these forces were the determining prin-ciples of its inner life. This is the sense in which we can say that the vegetative soul governs during the first time of life, the auto-motive soul governs during the second, and the sensitive soul or potency governs during the third. And this is the sense in which we can say that, for example, the primordial time in the life of the earth was the magnetic, from which it went over to the electric (and many things similar to this).

All life has only one law, and the same thing holds true with respect to the highest life. The same primordial forces that, when together, are (by nature) the principles of the inner life of the divinity – when these same forces emerge externally as potencies or with decision, they are the governing powers of the different times. Or stated generally: *the succession of potencies acts as a succession of times,* and vice versa.

With this law, opposition exhibits its rightful superiority and shows itself to be just as unconditional as unity. For while unity proves to be the governing principle throughout the expressed, it is subordinated to opposition in the expressing; there, opposition enjoys a freedom that cannot be overcome.

It is beyond dispute that the Eternal exists only by means of its free will; that is, through a free deed, it posits itself as existing. But granting this, the particular sequence of revelation the Eternal will choose does *not* depend on its freedom. This is the case even though the Eternal could have chosen not to reveal itself at all. If it wanted the final goal to be the revelation of itself, then the given sequence was necessary. And it was precisely the will that did not want revelation that had to be posited at the beginning. If the sequence had run in the opposite direction, everything would have ended in nonrevelation or in a revelation that would have been annulled again. What precedes in [the order of] revelation is not for that reason intrinsically subordinate; but if it is posited as subordinated, its successor is posited as higher in relation. Priority stands in an inverse relation to superiority: these concepts could only be confused by an error of judgment, and yet the tendency toward such an error is exemplified in our times.

The negating, enclosing will must precede in [the order of] revelation so there could be something to bear the grace [Huld] of the divinity and to carry it upward; for otherwise this grace would not be able to reveal itself. Wrath must come before love, severity before mildness, strength before gentleness. When the Lord passed before the prophet in a nocturnal vision, there was first a mighty storm that tore up the mountains and broke open the cliffs; then came an earthquake and finally a fire. But the Lord was himself in none of these; yet there followed a soft rustling, and he was in this. Likewise, violence, severity and power must precede in the revelation of the Eternal; and only then can he himself appear on the gentle breeze of love.

All development presupposes envelopment. In attraction there is beginning, and the fundamental force of contraction is in fact the original force, the root force of nature. All life begins with contraction; for why does everything progress from small into large and from narrow into wide when, if it were only a matter of progression, it could just as well be the other way around?

Darkness and concealment are the dominant characteristics of the primordial time. All life first becomes and develops in the night; for this reason, the ancients called night the fertile mother of things and indeed, together with chaos, the oldest of beings [Wesen]. The deeper we return into the past, the more we find unmoving rest, indistinction, and indifferent coexistence of the very forces that, though gentle at the beginning, flare up later into ever more turbulent struggle. The mountains of the primordial world seem to look down upon the animated life at their feet with eternally mute indifference; and likewise with the oldest formations of the human spirit. We encounter the same character of

concealment in the mute solemnity of the Egyptians, as well as in
the immense monuments of India, monuments that seem built
for no time but rather for eternity. Indeed, this character even
emerges in the silent grandeur and sublime tranquillity of the
oldest works of Hellenistic art, works that still bear within themselves the (albeit softened) force of that pure, noble age of the
world. Only in this way is there progress, only in this way is there
immortal life. If there were no decision, then there would only be
mute eternity and God without revelation. For this reason, it is
essential to insist that the forces are equally important. This is
countered often enough by the claim that the ideal is necessarily
higher than the real, and both cannot be equal. We have most
definitely acknowledged this relation by showing that the real is
always posited as the first potency, and the ideal as the higher,
second potency. But this cannot sublate the original equipollence.

If one of the two forces were by nature necessarily subordinated to the other, then there would be no freedom in God; nor
would there be progressive life. For let someone accept subordination as necessary, and hence as original; and let him, from the
very beginning, subordinate what is fundamentally determined
to the higher force! What would he have? He would be finished;
nothing more would be needed, no further progression, no
development. There is contradiction only because there is no *necessary* subordination; and only because there is contradiction is
there decision or freedom.

We will now enter the way of times and begin the description
of the first time and of the outwardly posited [herausgesetzten],
negating will.

When this will was at rest, it was in eternity, neither affirming
nor negating. Drawn from the outside and aroused to action, it
became a negating will, opposing the outside. But an outwardly
negating will would necessarily become an inwardly (or in itself)
affirming will, a will that willed revelation. This contradiction
required a decision. It is decided by an exuberant deed. There are
no longer two wills; there is only one. Moreover, this one will is
entirely unconditioned, never having decided to be the one and
not to be the other. Not that it posited the other will, but in con-

cealment; on the contrary, it is the active negation of the other. When a will is divided or in doubt, there is no decision. For this reason, the one will cannot simply not posit the other will; rather, it must absolutely negate this other will and posit that it is not.

The will that was originally neither affirmed nor negated but was, as such, simply inward – this will is now external; it has been posited outwardly as an actual will. But precisely because it is external, it stops being a conscious will and becomes a completely blind will that does not know itself.

Here is the point where even common conceptions touch upon our presentation. It is customary to represent the Revelation or the Creation of God as an externalization or as a descent [Herablassung] of the Eternal. This is how we have presented it as well. The force through which the divinity is genuinely in itself gets posited through revelation at the beginning. This force could not be overcome if it were to deny itself and remain in concealment; it renders itself amenable to overcoming by revealing itself and becoming external. The Eternal takes that part of its essence which – although not in fact the less significant – it is freely persuaded by love to regard as the less significant and makes it into the very innermost and strongest force at the beginning of existence [Daseyn]. The Eternal leads the force of the highest consciousness into unconsciousness and sacrifices it to externality so that there might be life and actuality.

This is how things had to stand if there were to be an eternal beginning, an eternal ground. That primordial deed which makes a man genuinely himself precedes all individual actions; but immediately after it is put into exuberant freedom, this deed sinks into the night of unconsciousness. This is not a deed that could happen once and then stop; it is a permanent deed, a never-ending deed, and consequently it can never again be brought before consciousness. For man to know of this deed, consciousness itself would have to return into nothing, into boundless freedom, and would cease to be consciousness. This deed occurs once and then immediately sinks back into the unfathomable depths; and nature acquires permanence precisely thereby. Likewise that will, posited once at the beginning and then led to the outside, must immediately sink into unconsciousness. Only in this way is a beginning possible, a beginning that does not stop being a beginning, a truly eternal beginning. For here as well, it is true that the beginning cannot know itself. That deed once done, it is done for all eternity. The decision that in some manner is truly to begin must not be brought back to consciousness; it must not be called back, because this would amount to being taken back. If, in making a decision, somebody retains the right to reexamine his choice, he will never make a beginning at all.

As we have said, that deed is done for eternity; that is, it is eternally what is done, and is consequently what has past. We thus see that by sinking into unconsciousness, the negating will is actually already acting as past – namely, for us. Already now, it works like something concealed, like that everlasting, eternal, primordial deed in us, even if it is not yet actually declared as such, and still less recognizes itself as such. Once drawn to the outside, led into unconsciousness, it does not know its own relation, it does not know that it is the preceding will, the ground of the future actuality of another will. Rather, the will is like the jealous God of the Old Testament, who tolerated no gods but himself, and his expression or word is this: I am the only one and there is no other but me.[1]

[1] [*Schelling's son appends the following explanation to the end of the text:* The manuscript prepared for printing does continue for another five or six pages, but a marginal note was added (by F. W. J. Schelling) that the treatise falls into utter falsehoods *from this point forward.* This self-critique explains why the author did not publish even the portion of the manuscript presented here. *The German editor adds the following explanation to the immediately preceding note:* An identical marginal note by Schelling's son appears after the concluding sentence of p. 178 above. The following two pages of the manuscript were crossed out. The two concluding pages were not crossed out; at the end of these pages, Schelling's son had copied out the concluding lines, together with the preceding marginal note. Further pages of the interrupted manuscript were not preserved, nor was the page with the original marginal note mentioned by Schelling's son.]